THE PACT

MY FRIENDSHIP WITH ISAK DINESEN

BY THORKILD BJØRNVIG

TRANSLATED FROM THE DANISH BY
INGVAR SCHOUSBOE AND
WILLIAM JAY SMITH
WITH AN INTRODUCTION BY
WILLIAM JAY SMITH

LOUISIANA STATE UNIVERSITY PRESS • BATON ROUGE AND LONDON

Designer: Barbara Werden
Typeface: Linotron Garamond #3
Typesetter: G&S Typesetters, Inc.

This book was published with the assistance of a grant-in-aid
from the Danish Ministry of Cultural Affairs and the Danish
Government Committee for Cultural Exchange.

LIBRARY OF CONGRESS CATALOGING IN PUBLICATION DATA

Bjørnvig, Thorkild.
The pact: my friendship with Isak Dinesen.

Translation of: Pagten.
1. Dinesen, Isak, 1885–1962—Friends and associates.
2. Bjørnvig, Thorkild—Friends and associates.   3. Authors,
Danish—20th century—Biography.   I. Title.
PT8175.B545Z5813   1983   839.8'1372   [B]   83-9335
ISBN 0-8071-1125-2

CONTENTS

THE PACT

INTRODUCTION

L IKE Thorkild Bjørnvig I read *Seven Gothic Tales* by Isak Dinesen when the book was first published to great acclaim in 1934. The stories seemed at once so classic and timeless and so unlike any others then being written that it was difficult to realize that the author was among the living. When this selection of the Book-of-the-Month Club appeared, American readers knew only that it was the work of a Continental European author writing in English. We learned soon that Isak Dinesen was in reality Baroness Blixen-Finecke of Rungstedlund near Copenhagen. Dinesen was her maiden name; Isak she had chosen because it meant "laughter" in Hebrew. A full-length photograph published after her identity became known showed an extremely slender woman in a long, flowing evening dress, her delicate but strong hands clasped on one hip, her heavy-lidded eyes nearly closed, a faint, almost mocking, smile on her lips. From her own account in *Out of Africa*, published in 1938, we discovered that Karen Blixen was quite as extraordinary as any tale she had told, that she had lived for seventeen years in Kenya, where she had run a coffee farm, hunted lions, walked with Masai warriors, and sat with Arab sheiks. While waiting for the rainy season in Africa, she had begun to put down some of the tales that she told to entertain a friend on his return from his safaris, one who had, she said, "a trait of character which to me is very precious, he liked to hear a story told." When the bottom dropped out of the coffee market, her farm was sold, and her friend, Denys Finch-Hatton, was killed when his small plane crashed. Having lost everything that was important to her, Karen Blixen returned to Denmark to begin a new life as the writer Isak Dinesen. With the publication of *Winter's Tales* in 1942 and the other books that followed until her death twenty years later, her worldwide reputation continued to grow. She was frequently mentioned as one of the leading contenders for the Nobel Prize for Literature; when Ernest Hemingway received it in 1954, he said that it should have gone to her. All her books were written while she was gravely ill, existing, we were told, largely on a diet of grapes, oysters, and champagne. In the twenty years since her death, her reputation has been strengthened by the publication of her essays and letters, by two biographies, and by several critical studies.

When in 1974 the distinguished Danish poet Thorkild Bjørnvig published *The Pact*, which was originally subtitled *My Friendship with Karen Blixen*, the book caused a sensation in Denmark. This record of the poet's intimate four-year association with the writer in the early 1950s presented a portrait unlike any other then known, and became immediately the center of controversy. Isak Dinesen had become such a legend in her lifetime that many readers welcomed this opportunity to have the veil pulled back and to see her revealed as she really was. Some readers hailed the book as a debunking of the public myth that Dinesen and her admirers had created. Others were outraged by what they considered a betrayal of the confidence that the old writer had placed in her young protégé; they found him as bumbling and uncouth as she had claimed at times he was. In their eyes, the picture that he painted was ugly, inconsiderate, and unnecessary. What relevance did all the unseemly personal details that he had unearthed have to do with her work that had long been established to be of enduring value? Although *The Pact* has been frequently mentioned in biographical and critical discussions of Isak Dinesen during the past ten years, no complete account of its contents appeared in English until Judith Thurman in 1982 published her comprehensive biography, *Isak Dinesen: The Life of a Storyteller*. The importance of *The Pact* in the Dinesen biography may be seen by the attention it receives in Judith Thurman's book: of the twenty final

chapters devoted to the last decade of Isak Dinesen's life, seven
are given over almost entirely to *The Pact*. Now with this translation American and English readers may judge for themselves
the validity of Thorkild Bjørnvig's account of the role he played
in the writer's life. Rather than being in any way a diminution
of her stature, *The Pact* will, I believe, show us in the person of
Karen Blixen a woman more passionate, vulnerable, and interesting than we had thought, and in Isak Dinesen a writer of even
greater power and subtlety than we had known. The book will
reveal, even in translation I trust, Thorkild Bjørnvig's own
considerable gifts. Those with no knowledge of the literary
background involved may still read *The Pact* as something akin
to a skillful and gripping novel.

I may well be one of the few people in this country who have
known both the principal characters in this extraordinary story
I met Thorkild Bjørnvig in 1978 at Norman, Oklahoma, when
we both served as judges, along with ten other writers and
critics from as many countries, to award the prestigious Neu-
stadt International Prize for Literature. This award of $25,000,
made every two years, is administered by *World Literature Today*
at the University of Oklahoma. Each juror presents a candidate:
mine was Eudora Welty and Thorkild Bjørnvig's was Nadezhda
Mandelstam; the prize in the end went to Czeslaw Milosz, who,
of course, was later to receive the Nobel Prize for Literature, as
did one of the other candidates, Elias Canetti. When I met him,
I knew nothing of Bjørnvig's friendship with Isak Dinesen. If I
had known, I would certainly have remarked on his apparent
predilection for indomitable women. The jurors decided that,
although Nadezhda Mandelstam, lacking a body of literary
work herself, did not exactly fit the category of writers meriting
the award, her extraordinary memoirs and the courage that she
had shown in keeping Osip Mandelstam's work alive under the
most difficult circumstances were indeed deserving of attention;

and we decided to give her a special citation. Isak Dinesen would certainly have been pleased by her protégé's efforts on the part of Mrs. Mandelstam: the latter embodied magnificently the courage that Dinesen thought had all but disappeared in the modern world.

Thorkild Bjørnvig impressed me at once as a man of great learning, who carried his learning lightly. His hair was completely white but his round, clear face was unlined and his blue eyes bright and sparkling. His dress was casual, and there was a remarkable openness about his nature. His buoyancy and youthful charm had not diminished with age, and he seemed to be enjoying himself immensely. I was struck, as Karen Blixen had been, by his resounding laugh. Like Emanuele in the story "Echoes," whom she modeled on him, "he might laugh for no apparent reason and apparently without being able to stop, like a kind of music box run riot." I found his laugh delightful, but I suppose if I had tried to analyze it, as Karen Blixen had, it might also have seemed puzzling. I got to know Thorkild Bjørnvig better when I went to visit him a few months later at Nordby on the island of Samsø, which lies almost at the geographical center of Denmark. There he lives with his beautiful wife Birgit in a charming house tucked away in the hills on the edge of the sea. I walked with him and his young son along the beach on a path not unlike the one he describes toward the end of *The Pact*. Then, and on my subsequent visits to Samsø and Copenhagen, we had long conversations on many subjects, including his friendship with Karen Blixen. We spent hours together putting into English his poem "The Dolphin," a splendid tribute to one of the greatest of living creatures, in language that is straightforward and powerful. I began to understand why, since the publication of his first book of love poems *Star Behind the Gable* in 1947, Thorkild Bjørnvig has come to be recognized as one of Denmark's foremost poets. Although he has published sparingly, each new work has received considerable critical attention, and his audience has grown. He has displayed tremendous virtuosity in all his work, from the sonnets on Nietzsche, which Karen Blixen admired, to a remarkable meditation on the death of Poe and a ballad about the Great Eastern. I began to understand also why critics had found his essays "refreshing and incisive and counter to the often sterile, 'hermetic' criticism practiced both in Denmark and elsewhere," and why his readers eagerly await the publication of the memoirs he is now completing. The confidence that Karen Blixen had in him was clearly not misplaced.

The exchange between the two characters in *The Pact* is like that in a Racinian drama or in the recitative of an opera. At moments of heightened tension there are extended declamations or arias. When the two tire of speaking themselves, they rise to play on the phonograph a song by Schubert or a symphony by Tschaikovsky. Both speakers are extraordinary because as writers both are conscious of the rhythm of their words and of the aural appeal that poetic language must have. For me the dialogue in *The Pact* is all the more affecting because I have heard the two real voices on numerous occasions, and because the author has recorded them here, with all their nuances, so admirably.

I heard the voice of Isak Dinesen (Karen Blixen)—or Tania, as she was known to her friends—for the first time at its full in 1959 when, in a black evening dress, her eyes dark with kohl, she sat on the stage at the Poetry Center of the YM-YWHA in New York and for an hour told her tales to a packed house, and told them without ever once referring to a page of paper or a book.

"I come from a long line of storytellers," she began in her rich and resonant contralto, and there was no question in the minds of her listeners that they were privileged to be in the presence of one of the great storytellers of modern times. That night she told two tales, "The Wine of the Tetrarch," an inset tale from

"The Deluge at Norderney," and "Barua a Soldani" (The King's Letter) about an episode on her African farm, later published in *Shadows on the Grass*.

Glenway Wescott has described her entrance at the Poetry Center that evening: "As she came on stage there, walking very slowly on the arm of a young staff poet named William Jay Smith, then pausing and turning and, by way of salute to the maximum audience including standees, outstretching her fine-boned arm in a gesture of some singularity—as of a hunter beckoning with a riding crop, or as of an actor in the role of Prospero motioning this or that airy creature into existence, or perhaps back out of existence—we all spontaneously stood up and acclaimed her.

"As soon as we kept quiet she established herself in an important straight chair, spot-lit, and after catching her breath in physical weariness for a moment, and gazing around the auditorium with a royal gaze, a gypsy gaze, began the evening's narration. She has an ideal voice for the purpose, strong, though with a kind of wraithlike transparency, which she is able to imbue with emotions, but only narrative emotions. She rarely indulges in mellifluousness in the way of poets; neither does she do much Thespian mimicking. . . . What especially colors Isak Dinesen's voice, what gives it overtone and urgency, is remembrance or reminiscence. With soft strong tone seeming to feel its way, sometimes almost faltering, shifting its direction, as power of evocation sways it, not perturbed by her listeners, perhaps helped by them, she seems to be re-experiencing what she has to tell, or if it is fable or fantasy, redreaming it."

There are no "staff poets" at the Poetry Center, but I had read my poems there, and Elizabeth Kray, who was then in charge of the programs, asked me to don a dinner jacket (unusual for the Center, where dress for poetry readings has usually been informal to the point of abandon) and to introduce the speaker, whose work she knew I admired. Never before or since have more pains been taken with arrangements. Ordinarily for a reading there are no preliminary preparations, nothing except perhaps a perfunctory testing of the microphone. We did not want to burden Baroness Blixen, ill and frail as she was, with any sort of rehearsal, but I was asked to come for a complete run-through. We checked out the lights, the placement of the Renaissance chair that Betty thought worthy of the occasion, and the small table accompanying it, on which was placed a glass of deep-gold vermouth. (Water was thought to be far too banal for such a Scheherazade.) Never had there been such preparations and never had there been such an audience. Her listeners came from every corner of Manhattan and from every walk of life—young writers who had just discovered her work, older members of the American Academy and Institute of Arts and Letters, which had elected her an honorary member and applauded her address at a dinner meeting, theatrical celebrities, and society women who had probably never before attended a reading of any sort. Taxis and limousines converged nonstop on Ninety-second Street: the evening had all the earmarks of the most glamorous Broadway opening. The reception was such that she was called back a second and then a third time to repeat the exact same program. A cartoon in the *New York Times Book Review* showed a beatnik in a Village haunt asking another, "Did you catch Isak Dinesen at the Y?" The *Times* also ran an advertisement of the kind that no speaker, not even Dylan Thomas, had received: ON MARCH 31ST. THIRD APPEARANCE BY DEMAND—ISAK DINESEN.

The year before, Barbara Howes, my former wife, had used the money that she had received from a Brandeis University Creative Arts Award to visit the Baroness at Rungstedlund, and the latter had been favorably impressed by her poetry. When she heard that I was to introduce her, I think she felt that she was in good hands, and she graciously invited Barbara and me to each

driver stop at a delicatessen, and provided them with a bag of chicken, ham, salad, and fruit. They were delighted, and laughed when I told them later that on my return to the party an elaborate meal had been served. While she may have eaten something late that night, most of the time she ate nothing at all, and ended up near death in the Harkness Pavilion. Once released, she continued her unrelenting pace. Just before the second of her New York readings, she received news of her sister's death in Denmark. That evening she seemed more intent than ever on appearing as a *memento mori*: she wore no make-up, a long black dress, and gypsy earrings, heavy silver loops that touched her shoulders. At Leo Lerman's party afterward, she noticed that one of the earrings, a gift from Denys Finch-Hatton, had disappeared. It was the only time that I saw her visibly distressed. A thorough search of the house and the car turned up nothing, but the earring was discovered when she returned to her room; it had slipped down into her dress.

Isak Dinesen's work is concerned with loss—the loss of Africa, the loss of Denys Finch-Hatton, the loss of her health, and the loss of what she considered civilized values in the modern world. She realizes almost as soon as she meets Thorkild Bjørnvig that she will lose him also. And yet she struggles passionately to hang on to him; and, in the end, is left, as in the classical drama, which she evokes, with only her passion. In her attempt to control him, she speaks in exalted, biblical language. She identifies with the gods, and becomes herself a goddess; or with the Devil, whose handmaiden she is. She attempts to change the pact of friendship into a covenant, sealed with blood, so that the friendship will become a union of the flesh as well as of the spirit, which she knows in reality it can never be. The whole affair degenerates into a *folie à deux*, and she suffers from the megalomania which she feared that her disease would bring on. With Pellegrina Leoni in "Echoes," she cries out in triumph when she finds the young disciple whose voice will replace hers, "I have got my talons in him. He will not escape me." But he does escape, as she knew he would.

And yet artistically he does not escape: he is there in her story "Echoes" for himself and for the world to see. Isak Dinesen remarked once in an interview that she was fortunate in possessing exceptionally keen senses and that she had never met anyone who could see as well as she could. As Thorkild Bjørnvig testifies, she could spot four-leaf clovers as she strolled along without having to kneel down in the grass. In her art also she is able to view her subject from a distance. She looks back on her life in Africa, her lost farm and her lost love, from a great height and brings them all close up. She looks back on the life of her own family and on the life that had preceded her in Denmark and in Europe; and she looks farther back on classical Greece and beyond. This vision gives her work a dimension almost totally lacking in modern writing. In a sense, hers was no idle boast that she was three thousand years old, a witch who had dined with Socrates.

Part and parcel of this artistic dimension is Isak Dinesen's extreme reticence. The story she gives us in *Out of Africa* is, as art, in every way complete. And yet when we read the wonderful letters that she wrote back from Kenya (and if only her letters remained, she would still command attention as a writer), we see how much she omitted. We accept her description of Finch-Hatton as a man of heroic proportions. Seen through her loving eyes, he had no failings, no flaws. From her book we know nothing of their misunderstandings, their quarrels, the quotidian aspects of their affair. The break that took place before Finch-Hatton's sudden death, and what led up to it, is not even mentioned. And rightly so, I believe, because it is not artistically germane: she is concerned only with detailing the lineaments and development of her passion and her loss. At one point in *The Pact* Karen Blixen remarks that she felt sometimes when she was together with Bjørnvig that it was like an echo of her time with Denys Finch-Hatton, "frailer but the same, the same." And in writing of this affair in "Echoes" she is as reticent as she was in *Out of Africa*. The poet is viewed from considerable distance; in the story the young man becomes a mere boy, her tale an echo of an echo. For anyone interested in Karen Blixen as a person (and unlike many writers she was a truly fascinating person), *The Pact* is invaluable. Because her relationship with Bjørnvig is a reflection of her affair with Finch-Hatton, we can gain from the reflection insight into the darker aspects of that earlier and more important involvement.

By putting down in *The Pact* what Isak Dinesen left out, Thorkild Bjørnvig has written more than a personal memoir. He is wrong, I think, when he tells us that he learned next to nothing from Karen Blixen about his craft as a poet but everything about life. Whatever else she taught him about writing, *The Pact* clearly shows that she taught him how to tell a story. Even for the reader unfamiliar with the work of Isak Dinesen, the book reads like a novel, detailing minutely the growth and decline of sentiment. By picking up the material that she chose to discard, Bjørnvig has perhaps written the novel that she never wrote. It calls to mind an epistolary novel of the eighteenth century: Bjørnvig and Blixen constantly communicate with each other by letter even when in the same house and if not by letter then by some other written document, a poem or a story. When not writing to each other, they are talking, analyzing how each stands to the other in terms of their pact. The book indeed recalls that classic novel of psychological analysis, *Adolfe*, written in 1807 by Benjamin Constant under circumstances not entirely unlike those at Rungstedlund. Constant, whose life was marked by liaisons with women older than himself, was for seventeen years the largely platonic companion of Mme. de Staël, one of the leading literary figures of the day, as indomitable as Karen Blixen but far less interesting. Her hold on Constant was such that not even the disclosure of his secret marriage to another woman would permit him to break with her. There was also, as with Bjørnvig and Blixen, a written pact of attachment. In that affair it was Constant who was syphilitic, and the advanced stage of the disease may have accounted for the peculiarity of some of his actions. Bjørnvig had only his youth and his unformed sensibility to blame, and the portrait he draws of himself as a young man is not always estimable. Readers of *The Pact* may feel that Bjørnvig, like Constant, suffered from abulia, that psychological impairment of the ability to decide or act independently. But whatever his failings, he had, like Constant, the honesty to put down *not* how he would liked to have been but how he actually was. And so in *The Pact* the truth, as he wished it, "speaks clean."

Karen Blixen told Thorkild Bjørnvig that she wanted the two of them to go down in literary history; and with *The Pact*, as with "Echoes," they will. She would have hated him for being at times in the writing of his book, as he had been when they were together, soft where she would have been hard, romantic where she would have been classical, solemn where she would have been playful, but because he has written, as she had begged him to, "entirely from the heart," she would surely in the end have approved of this remarkable document and would have given it her blessing.

WILLIAM JAY SMITH

TRANSLATORS' NOTE

W ITH the author's approval, a few brief deletions have been made in the original text. These have usually involved material containing the names of Danish literary or historical figures unfamiliar to the American or English reader. In the opening chapters two letters that the author was unable to locate at the time of the original writing have been added. In a few other places slight changes have been made in the wording. None of these minor alterations, deletions, or additions has in any way changed the basic intent of the original text.

Notes deemed necessary to identify certain of the author's references have been made as brief and as unobtrusive as possible.

The translators are grateful to Helen Handley and Leif Sjöberg for their careful review of the translation and to Elizabeth Sisco and Elisabeth Hayward for assistance in the preparation of the manuscript.

The author and translators wish to thank Parmenia Migel, author of the pioneering biography of Isak Dinesen, for generously allowing the use of several of her valuable photographs of Isak Dinesen; also Frans Larson, who arranged for use of photographs from the Royal Library of Copenhagen.

THE PACT IS MADE ✿ ✿ ✿ ✿

A S AN undergraduate I had read *Seven Gothic Tales* and
Winter's Tales by Isak Dinesen (Karen Blixen). I knew
nothing about the author; who she was concerned me no more
than who might have told the tales of *The Arabian Nights* or the
Grimm *Fairy Tales*. I did not in fact think that she was among
the living, and I was quite astonished when Ole Wivel suggested that we get in touch with her when he and I began our
search for contributors to the magazine *Heretica*.* He even knew
her personally. It seemed fantastic to me that Karen Blixen was
alive and perhaps might contribute to the periodical, as Ole
Wivel seemed to think was not impossible. In June 1947 we
decided to visit her to present our plans, but she happened to be
out of the country. It was not until the winter of 1948 that I
finally met Karen Blixen for the first time.

I received one day quite unexpectedly an invitation from her
to a small dinner party in the winter quarters of her house at
Rungstedlund. Karen Blixen wrote that her niece, Countess
Caritas Bernstorff-Gyldensteen, was absolutely enchanted with
my poems and wanted very much to meet me. When I read the
invitation I became slightly dizzy; I was to meet my first real
reader, one who even wanted to meet me and had said so;
moreover, one who was the daughter of a count and a niece of the

---

* *Heretica* (1948–1953) was edited in 1948–49 by Thorkild Bjørnvig and
Bjørn Poulsen; in 1950–51 by Ole Wivel and Martin A. Hansen; and in
1952–53 by Frank Jaeger and Tage Skou-Hansen. The periodical, which was
anti-ideological, revolted against the narrow intellectualism of twentieth-
century culture and put its main stress on art as humanity's purest and noblest
expression. Ole Wivel (1921–   ), author, teacher, and close friend of Thorkild Bjørnvig, has been since 1973 director of the Gyldendal Publishing
House. —Tr.

Baroness! I paused, overcome with excitement; it was as if the door had been thrown wide open to the great world; soon I would stand on the threshold of fame and adventure: I was to be *lionized*. I slept little that night; several times I pulled on my rubber boots and in my pajamas paced about in the cold thicket under the big trees to cool my burning expectations.

The next evening I cycled to Rungstedlund, where I was shown in and introduced to Karen Blixen, her brother Thomas Dinesen, and to the Countess and her family. The ladies wore long dresses as for a formal party, and that seemed a bit unusual in the relatively small winter quarters, as if a ballroom had suddenly been telescoped into a magic box. After sherry and salted almonds, we went into dinner and I was placed next to the lady of my dreams. The Countess was stately and amiable, and the situation, as well as the sherry, on top of the cold bicycle trip, went a bit to my head.

After we were seated and Karen Blixen had left the room for a moment, the Countess quickly leaned over and whispered, "I regret that I have not yet had time to read your poems. I'm very sorry, for Tanne (the nickname for Karen Blixen that was used by her relatives and close friends) lent them to me and told me to be sure to read them before this evening. Please, don't tell her that I haven't." My first reader! But I promised not to tell and had no trouble not speaking of it to Karen Blixen. I felt more than odd sitting there, slightly spinning, as if I had stumbled over the threshold to fame instead of making a dignified entry and now had to get to my feet as discreetly as possible. That was greatly facilitated by the fact that the Countess was happily ignorant of my expectations, and suddenly I felt the situation to be completely relieved and burst out in heartwarming laughter. From then on we ate and drank and carried on an excellent conversation about everything under the sun, except my poems. When the evening was over, Karen Blixen invited me to come again soon.

The following spring I moved with my wife and two-year-old son into a prefabricated Finnish frame house across a clearing from Bjørn Poulsen's log cabin, a few kilometers inland from Vedbaek. To this little spot called "Bjørnebo," Karen Blixen often came, walking or cycling, to have tea with my wife and me and sometimes to play with our little son. Under the spell of her presence, he would occasionally perform peculiar dances. Once she exclaimed: "Doesn't he look just like Ophelia in the mad scene?" There was no subject we did not touch on in our conversations, and she repeated her invitation to come to Rungstedlund. From this time on, I went to see her quite frequently and eventually she said that for me the door would always be open; I could literally just walk in. Later in our friendship she amplified her invitation: I could disturb her at any time, even at night, by tossing pebbles at her window, if I had something pressing that I needed to discuss with her. I never dared—and never found the occasion—to accept this generous offer.

When I reached Rungstedlund, I often found her sitting on an upholstered bench, her legs pulled up beneath her, turned sideways to the window behind her, listening to records. This was always in the winter quarters of her house, and I think she stayed there that entire year. I would sit down and listen to the music without knowing if she had noticed me. I would gaze at her long, sorrowful profile against the spring light or the winter dusk. Perhaps she ignored my presence only while the music lasted, but it sometimes happened that she exclaimed with surprise that she had not heard me come in.

On one of my early visits, she showed me Frederik Schyberg's review* of *Seven Gothic Tales*, about which she was deeply indignant. Neither flattery nor objective appraisal could assuage her feelings. I wondered how this single review could be so much on

* Karen Blixen often showed a copy of this young critic's review, published in *Berlingske Tidende*, to her friends as an example of the Danish mentality that was incapable of appreciating her work. —Tr.

the mind of this wise and famous author, this woman of the
world. Now I know that even the greatest artists, almost without exception, can be upset by such criticism. I took the review
home with me and wrote to her shortly afterwards:

> I have studied Schyberg's fantastic review, the ex-
> pression of a Puritan soul in uproar, his voice almost
> quavering with righteousness, deep indignation, and a
> feeling of swimming against the tide. But be that as it
> may, his review may have its own logic. One cannot
> demand of the true critic that he be a mere chameleon,
> that he combine his personal bias with unconditional
> many-sidedness. However that may be, it does seem
> depressing and unpleasant that he seeks his starting
> point not in the book but outside it, and hence arrives
> at an almost blasphemous distortion and at an extreme
> indignation that is heartrending. His starting point,
> Baroness, seems to be you yourself, and the praise of the
> American reviewers, which for him gets in the way of
> the book. To be honest, if I had come to *Seven Gothic
> Tales* preconditioned by his review, I think I would have
> been deeply suspicious of it. Today it is extremely rare,
> if not unheard of, for a book of genuine value to attain a
> public success comparable to that of *Seven Gothic Tales*. I
> believe that its success is due to certain characteristics
> (over and above its quality), which Schyberg would
> interpret as catering to public taste, although they most
> certainly do not. The most profound parts of Goethe's
> *Werther* did not bring about its success, no more than
> the triumph of *Seven Gothic Tales* can be ascribed to its
> wisdom. I even feel that Schyberg is right when he lists
> the qualities that brought about the book's acclaim: the
> romantic, mystical aura surrounding everything, the

magic of the names, the aristocratic setting. But Schyberg has seen nothing but these, and is wholly insensitive to the central wisdom that shines throughout, particularly in tales such as "The Dreamers" and "The Deluge at Norderney." The British and American reviewers seem to me to have fundamentally the same shortcomings; they usually deal, as Schyberg does, only with superficial aspects, they in praise, he in holy indignation. I am happy that I experienced your book with the same innocence, clarity, and strength as when I encountered Shelley, Poe, and Baudelaire for the first time, without joy or embarrassment because of knowing you personally or because of any rave reviews or literary hatchet jobs. If I ever write about your books, I shall return to this powerful first impression as my pure source of inspiration.

Karen Blixen possessed a special kind of genius. Great talent was, of course, one of its indispensable qualities, but certainly not the only one; only in its organic combination with the rest of her person—mind and body, senses and heart—did talent manifest itself as genius. And apparently it was only in evidence temporarily, under special circumstances, like rare animals or plants. Suddenly it was present, acted and had its effect, and suddenly it was gone. It reminded one of wisdom, but lacked what otherwise is characteristic of wisdom, namely invulnerability and continuity. Almost X-ray-like it would see through the conditions for being and growth in other persons, but abruptly and without transition it would jump from action on their conditions to action on her own. She could with all her heart yearn for responsibility and consistency, but she found it almost unbearable to practice them except in her conduct toward her servants and toward animals. "I wish people would regard me as insane," she would complain. "It would be such a relief."

Because Karen Blixen was a woman of sixty-four when I met her (precisely twice as old as I was at the time) and frequently ill, I experienced this special genius mostly in conversations. As our mutual confidence and spiritual exchange grew with each meeting, one afternoon, as we were strolling in the park and had had an exceptionally good conversation, almost perfectly harmonious in its perceptions, she said that I should not write the book about her work which she had originally suggested to me. "That is not the reason we met," she said. "No, we have met for an entirely different reason. I realize that now, and I will tell you one day about it."

Our conversations would usually move from matters concerning contemporary poets and my magazine to more general topics such as Eros and Christianity, animals and the cosmos, the war and vivisection, and our often unexpected and spontaneous agreement did not stop the conversation as so often happens—but simply guided it quickly past all nonessentials, and, as if by mighty inertia, into a kind of happy, productive dimension. Above all, she did not tire of impressing on me the necessity of courage, which she felt was held in low esteem at that time. "Everybody is so unhappy because courage is counted for nothing. People today are brought up to be anything but courageous. To be courageous is neither proper nor fashionable. And so no one can be truly happy, for then one must also run the risk of becoming really unhappy, and that, I believe, nobody is. No, it takes courage to be happy. And this you must promise me: never to be afraid, for then you cannot be happy. And what is there to be afraid of?" she concluded with provocative emphasis. It seemed to me that she touched the very base of my being and swept aside masses of opinions, concepts, and layers of prejudices I did not suspect I had. To be with her and converse with her was an experience that crossed boundaries and opened up the world. When I left her, whether in the intense light of the early spring evening or in rainy darkness along the seashore, I often felt intoxicated with a tremendous expectation of life, greater than I had ever known before. It was like meeting a person of a kind I had heard about in myth and history, and this impression was in keeping with my having originally believed that she was no longer living. Now I certainly felt her living presence, to say the least. On her side, she developed an unusual trust and confidence in me, which I did not understand, but which I reciprocated unconditionally.

I expressed my emotion and gratitude in a letter written to her on January 20, 1950, the same day she had given a lecture which my wife and I attended. Karen Blixen had often spoken of her loneliness, the loss of her servant Farah,* and of the absence of kindred spirits around her. I thought the moment had come when I might simply offer to serve her. I wrote:

Dear Baroness Blixen,

The stars were large and close to earth and twinkled in the cold last night as we walked home across the fields. It was as if your eyes and your words had drawn them closer. As I walked, I thought of you, of the evening, of the many evenings I have listened to you and conversed with you. Last night was like a long wonderful monologue at a symposium, a monologue about the secrets and the unpredictability of life, a monologue about Eros, eliciting laughter and tears. Who but you could create such a symposium now that the symposium has become impossible? Who but you could speak to an assembly as if it were made up solely of equals, of beautiful people? If I told my friends or colleagues about all this, they

* Karen Blixen's majordomo in Kenya. —Tr.

tion turned to Nietzsche, whose *Thus Spake Zarathustra* she had loved since her youth. "Because you know Nietzsche so well," she said, "you must tell me if you have found or now find signs of megalomania in me of the kind he had. And if you do see such signs you must warn me as soon as possible; you really owe me that, it is part of our pact; you must defend my honor."

IN PARIS ✍ ✍ ✍ ✍ ✍ ✍ ✍

D URING the two years that I edited *Heretica*, I translated
several poems and essays by modern European authors
and wrote a book on Martin A. Hansen,* the only author about
whom Karen Blixen and I seriously disagreed. But I was not
writing poetry, which I was burning to do and which I felt I had
to do. I grew weary of the editorial meetings and discussions
among *Heretica*'s contributors, who often felt annoyed not just
by what others wrote in the periodical but by their having been
allowed to write in it at all. Each one harbored his own particular dissatisfaction, and so, to a great degree, did Karen Blixen
herself. We talked of all this, and she wrote to me on October 6,
1949: "Sometimes I am afraid that the Heretics [as the contributors to the magazine were called] are about to become somewhat like the Pre-Raphaelites. The Pre-Raphaelites were competent but dreadful people; they make any viewer want to give
up painting completely."

Contributions to the magazine kept pouring in, often followed by the most peculiar insults when work had been rejected. Reading contributions and answering the authors had
turned me away from the writing of poetry or made what poetry
I did write seem to me of no value whatever. Karen Blixen
decided that I needed to get away, and she suggested that my
wife and I go to Paris in the spring. The experience of a spring in
Paris she regarded as an indispensable part of my European
education. I applied at the university for a traveling scholarship
and was successful. I planned to spend about a year in France. I
resigned my position as editor, and in April 1950 my wife and I

---

* Martin A. Hansen (1905–1955), novelist, short-story writer, and essayist, is considered one of the greatest Danish writers of the twentieth century
and a major influence on other writers. —Tr.

went to Paris, where we stayed at the Cité Universitaire for the
next three months.

It was a cold spring and in that sparkling but semidecayed
city, full of so much that was absolutely strange to me, I encountered immediately the traditional French scorn for any
foreigner who does not speak almost perfect French. I set out to
learn the language but found it frustrating. Karen Blixen probably thought my progress in Paris was too slow, and when I
complained of the language difficulty (foreign languages have
never been easy for me to learn), I received late in April a long
letter in which she wrote, among other things, that she perhaps
had had too much respect for my university degree: "I did not
think it would be so hard for you to learn French. If I had, I
would in time have beseeched you to step down and sit on the
school bench instead of traveling around to mount lecterns and
recite poetry. Now I am sorry that I did not do just that. If you
were not married to Grete, I would pass on to you the good
advice my father gives in one of his *Letters from the Hunt* (*Jagt-
breve*), 'Il faut coucher [*sic*] avec son dictionnaire.'" At first I
naively took this literally. In my boyhood I had heard that the
most difficult school books should be placed under one's pillow
just before an examination for some mystical strengthening of
one's memory during sleep. Her letter concluded:

> I hope you can feel that behind Mentes' perhaps slightly
> pedantic admonitions it is really Athena who speaks,
> she who has pleaded your cause in the assembly of the
> gods. I myself will hasten to Ithaca so that my words
> may encourage the beloved young man and kindle
> courage in his breast . . . because it becomes you poorly
> to behave like a child. Your childhood days are over.
> . . . So, my dear, be bold! Since I see that you are
> handsome and grown-up, be bold so that you may
> be praised by future generations!

Naturally the letter made me very happy. I felt honored but also quite ashamed, and after reflecting for some time, I wrote to her at the beginning of May:

> I understand that I have irritated you greatly and not for the first time. These first letters are no doubt to some degree a mixture of dementia praecox and hubris, but now I believe my period of initiation is over and I am ready for this city. I have natural talents really for nothing in this world; my slowness of perception is almost extraordinary and I wonder whether Mrs. Carlsen* wasn't right when she, in a sudden moment of insight, insinuated that Thorkild Bjørnvig was hardly as gifted as the Baroness thought. The point is that far from having buried my one small talent in a fit of hurt feelings, I have, on the contrary, vigorously and industriously made the most of it and I think I have made good progress in both speaking and reading French.

Karen Blixen must have felt nonetheless that I behaved too much like a child and that I did not take her admonitions seriously enough. A short time afterwards I had a concussion, and later Karen Blixen sincerely felt that she had caused it. One afternoon, feeling suddenly a total loss of patience with me, she banged her fist on the table and exclaimed: "May this blow strike the Magister† on his head!" And it so happened that she did this at the very instant that I ran into a sharp edge in my room. It could have been a great joke, but she did not look on it as such: no, it was a small curse that should have had the character of a reproof. But when she later saw the long-term

* Karen Blixen's housekeeper at Rungstedlund. —Tr.

† Magister designates a person holding the Danish academic degree of Magister (roughly the equivalent of our Master's). Karen Blixen often referred to the author, even addressed him, by this title. It was another decade before he received his Ph.D. —Tr.

consequences of her curse, she deeply regretted that her blow had apparently been so severe. That was not her intention. In the beginning I passed off the whole thing as nothing and could not believe that something as idiotic as a concussion, however slight, should happen to me there in Paris, on the seventeenth of May, now that spring had finally arrived in all its gentle splendor and now that the disturbing and moving enchantment of the city was at long last beginning to take hold of me. So I thoroughly neglected my head and paid no attention to warnings until I was laid low.

When Karen Blixen heard this, she wrote a beautiful letter to my wife, but it was three weeks before I heard from her directly. She must meanwhile have gone over everything in her mind. Her letter to me was a long one, written with beak and claws, in love and anger, full of deep insight. Dated June 6, 1950, it was a continuation of our conversations after the establishment of the pact:

> My not having written to you does not mean that I have not thought of you; my thoughts have often been in Paris. If Grete received my letter, you can see how sad I have been to hear about your concussion. I do hope you have recovered completely by now.
>
> I'll put down some of the things I have thought about in connection with you. Do not let the random order bother you, it will be as if we were sitting and talking to each other. It's rather sad that you are not here to respond.
>
> You say that you suppose that you have annoyed me thoroughly several times and I will tell you right away that you have indeed vexed me and that you are going to do it again, perhaps even disappoint me, when you demonstrate that Mrs. Carlsen was right. But absolutely nothing in this world can at any time make any

change whatever in my friendship for you. It is with you as with Farah. In the wedding ritual itself it is written, and it must be meant seriously, "Till death do us part." When I received a letter that Farah had died, that did not change him for me, although the world which may await us after death looked suddenly different. Neither is anything changed in the pact between us.

Do you remember how once you escorted me part way home from Bjørnebo? The snow was deep on the trail and Pasop* pursued a hare? That was when I told you about Heiberg's puppet play, *The Potter*. In this comedy, the young woman Rosa says to the hero who is in a terrible situation:

Now if you have lost your faith in God,
believe in me, and I will give you shelter.

That was intended as more than just a quotation, and I believe it was so understood.

It takes something to say this, to make this offer, if I may call it that. Here I return to Farah: he made me that offer, not just when he became my majordomo, although then as well. During my first year in Africa, there was a time when Farah and my other servants, all things in Africa, and Africa itself said the same thing to me:

Believe in us, and we will give you shelter.

Africa is, of course, somewhat greater than I am, and has been around a few thousand years longer, but the importance of the offer lies not in that. Pasop could also have made it. It also takes something to accept it. At that time I accepted Africa's offer with all my strength,

* Karen Blixen's German shepherd. —Tr.

and that was why it became a pact between us, "in which there was no change, no shadow of vicissitude."

The motto of the Finch-Hattons on their coat of arms is: "*Je responderay*," [I will answer], which I like very much. It contains a decision: to be as good as one's word, as well as the expression of an ability or a talent; that one is *able to respond*, that one has a sounding board, a preparedness, as an echo of one's mind.

In Heiberg's play Rosa is a simple, humble person, like Pasop. And Farah was always my servant. None of them would dream of taking the place of God or even of temporarily substituting for Him. No, they were just able to avert a person's eyes from people—in Potter Walter's case also from the mine owner himself—to the gods.

Do you remember I said that I loved wild animals more than tame ones? That I thought the former more respectable because unlike the latter they have a direct relationship to God? Consider ducks in a duck pond; they are busy but one can see no direction to their activity. But then gaze at wild ducks crossing the skies! How conscious of their goal they are! Yes, so much so that we who look up at them from the ground and have no way of knowing their goal can perceive and acknowledge it. Their flight is exactly like the flight of an arrow. That is also why I think Hubert is the only respectable character in *The Riding Master* (*Rytteren*).*

---

*In *Isak Dinesen: The Life of a Storyteller* Judith Thurman says that *The Riding Master* (*Rytteren*) by Hans Christian Branner, published in 1949, "was consumed with almost universal delight by the Danish public and achieved, almost immediately, the status of a modern classic. Karen Blixen took the story very personally and identified with the fate of its central character, a centaur. She also sat down to write a critique of it, addressed in a sincere and personal voice to the author himself. . . . Briefly, the story concerns four

He, at least, has a direct relationship to God—or perhaps to the Devil—and so can stick by himself. The others are extremely busy and talk an awful lot, but one sees no direction to their activity.

The dignity of a human being lies in his having a direct relationship to the gods. The dignity of lions and giraffes lies in the direct relationship they have to some African deity, perhaps unknown to us. Therefore it is terrible to put them into zoos and to place people, however well-meaning, between them and their gods. Thus the grandees of Spain had a direct relationship to their King; the prouder they were, the prouder the King was of them. It was to the honor of the King of Spain that he had servants so proud that they had the right to keep their hats on in his presence.

What I now wish for you in Paris is this: that while you move freely and easily among people, you still feel your own being to be as whole as a giraffe's or an elephant's on the plains, as independent and unchallengeable. That you should have no "face value" set by people, but find your full value in and of yourself.

If you have only a face value, what are you good for? You can be in circulation and be useful for a purpose; you can go lock, stock and barrel into a business or an enterprise, but you can give nothing of yourself. The smallest piece of a genuine gold coin, even the dust scraped from it, is always gold, but a corner or even a

---

characters who have all known and in different ways fallen under the spell of a riding master named Hubert. He is dead, trampled by a horse, and this was either an accident or a murder, for several of the characters claim to have killed him. But none of them can forget him and, indeed, the novel is a series of conversations in which they argue, lament, execrate, revere, and struggle with his memory." —Tr.

half of a one hundred kroner bill is nothing; less than a blank piece of paper, which at least you can write on.

I said in my last letter that you had been pampered too much. I did not mean to say that you had been over praised or flattered. That, I am reasonably sure, is not the case, but I think you have been looked at too much just as unhappy spoiled children are. Often there is something like varnish in the eyes of people that seals the pores of the skin of the one looked at against air and light.

I remember that Jakob Knudsen* says of the starry skies:

> What omnipotent innocence!
> Mighty enough to drown the public observing eye
> in the eternally unseen!

What I reckon to be a kind of pact between you and me is to me serious to such a degree that I have been reluctant to talk much about you since you left. But people have talked about you to me. They often say, "We hope he keeps at his writing." It is as if they sat around you observing, waiting for you to lay an egg! I certainly want you to give all that you have to give at some time, but above all, I want right now that you really feel and know that you are alive. Keats said, "Shakespeare led a life of allegory; his works are comments on it."

Soon afterward, Karen Blixen arrived quite unexpectedly to visit us. I had recovered somewhat and was delighted to be with her again. I took her visit to be a seal of approval and the consummation of my stay in France, which, apart from my mishap, had by that time fully lived up to all my expectations.

*Jakob Knudsen (1858–1917) was a clergyman, religious essayist, novelist, and writer of hymns. —Tr.

Karen Blixen stayed at the St. James and Albany, where we usually visited her in her room before we went out to dinner together. On the first occasion, while we were going down in the elevator, we got stuck between two floors. The elevator had doors almost entirely of glass at both ends and there we stood, the three of us as in a fishbowl, looking out over the enormous lobby through one of the doors, signaling as best we could. A tall ladder was brought up at once to the door that faced the lobby. This was done in an amazingly routine fashion and so quickly it seemed as if the ladder had been ready and waiting. As it turned out, it was indeed kept in readiness, for this was not the first time that the elevator had failed to function; it happened every week. We got out, the Baroness last, with great dignity, like a great bird that decides not to fly down so as not to cause an unnecessary disturbance. The evening was a festive one with dinner at a famous old restaurant, in which, under other circumstances, I would not have dared to set foot, with culinary delights far surpassing my understanding and experience, but not beyond my ecstatic appreciation.

The next day Karen Blixen visited us in our room at the Cité Universitaire. It was a beautiful and spacious top-floor room with a dormer window and a magnificent view. She enjoyed herself, talked at length, smoked, and drank cups of tea. In the course of the conversation she took from her purse a poem that she said had been written by her nephew Tore Dinesen, and asked my opinion of it. I read it carefully several times, wondering how a young man in this day and age could think of writing as he did. When Karen Blixen emphasized that she wanted my honest evaluation even though the writer was her nephew, I gave it to her. My rather devastating criticism was delivered in a polite but irritated fashion, as if I had to take advantage of the opportunity to get at all the impossible contributions I had received as an editor. And furthermore, with the intolerance and the unconsciously rejecting arrogance that so easily grips a poet when he is in a creative period, as I then was, I found it utterly hopeless: pastiche, inversions, conventional rhymes and rhythm devoid of any tension, even though it was moving, particularly the last stanza. She took it all very nicely, considering that she had written it herself, as I found out later. Today the poem may be read in "Ib and Adelaide," where it occurs as Adelaide's dirge and the context fully justifies the pastiche. Not so with the poem itself. It has the effect of something deeply personal, like indelible drops of blood from a mournful heartache, as insurmountable as Adelaide's, but having come from an entirely different situation. This is in keeping with the fact that in the story the recollection of the poem is described as an assault on Adelaide from the subconscious. This and the unassimilated personal features are typically modernistic traits in the story. Karen Blixen was like other prose writers who have tried their hand at poetry; they are almost always more in tune with modern times in their prose than in their poems.

The next time Karen Blixen paid us a visit in our room, I read aloud to her "Leda," which is now the second section in my long poem "The Raven" (*Ravnen*). The first I had read to her at Rungstedlund. She studied it for a long time and said she found it very beautiful. She added that because I had obeyed the poem's visible and also its unwritten laws, my description of the passionate naked embrace had become noble and powerful art and not mere pornography. I had got a spontaneity and sureness in the movements like a tightrope walker who, no more than I, would transgress his laws of movement with a fall. And she went on, picking up a thread from her last letter almost verbatim, and said that if I really wanted to write she would wholeheartedly wish me good luck and happiness. "Do not write for any one person, or for *Heretica*, or for any movement or cultural issue. Write because you owe the gods an answer. *Je responderay*," she said, concluding with the motto of the Finch-Hattons. Her remarks made a deep impression on me. Nothing could better fit the thoughts I had about "The Raven," the dizzying plan in my head and the aim of the poem. Whatever "The Raven" has become since then, I have obeyed her admonition, and it shows, if in no other way, in that it apparently is almost inaccessible to most readers.

On her last afternoon in Paris, Karen Blixen hired a convertible and took us for a long tour of the Bois de Boulogne. She treated me like a patient and told us many things about the Bois. She spoke of the great hunt that Napoleon the Third had held for many foreign guests and how for this occasion several hundred large multicolored parrots had been turned loose in the woods, all trained to scream, "Vive l'Empereur!" and how, under steady fire from the foreign diplomats, they had died for their emperor with this scream issuing from their beaks. With the greening trees in the mild spring air, I could, in my euphoric condition, clearly visualize the whole scene, and I laughed and enjoyed myself as if intoxicated. When Karen Blixen was in the mood, she could give an exalted grotesque twist and accent to everything she described, augmented by such an imperturbable deadpan mien that I could not stop laughing. Once again she inquired about our travel plans. (We were going first to Brittany and then to the Mediterranean.) She issued her last bit of advice, concluding: "I am sorry that I have to leave, but I am also happy about it. It is always like that. I see that I can let you go, and bless you, at least for a while. I hope that it will be a time of happiness for you, for both of you." The next day she flew back to Denmark and my parents-in-law arrived, bringing our three-year-old son. After a week of sightseeing in Paris, we all went by train to Brittany, where we had rented rooms for a month at the Hôtel l'Etoile des Mers, at Saint-Cast-l'Isle.

The hotel faced the Atlantic and stood up against a sheer cliff. We had obtained a room with an unobstructed view of the ocean. I was still in a condition of unstable convalescence, and to borrow a phrase of Morten Nielsen's,* "My joy was skating on thin ice." But I had every reason to hope that I would get well in this large unspoiled marine landscape. It did not turn out that way. Former guests of the hotel arrived the next day and wanted a room facing the ocean, and in spite of our agreement of several months' standing, the woman who ran the hotel used the fact that we had a child as an excuse to move us to a room at the rear, facing the cliff. There a pathetic-looking lantern shone into the room at night unless we drew the curtains and perished from the heat. The room was located just above the kitchen and our door opened onto the back stairs. The manager cared nothing about breaking our agreement. When we brought the inconvenience to her attention, she treated us like bums. Sleep and health were lost on the hot stuffy nights with smells and noise emanating early and late from the kitchen. Everything along the coast was either booked or occupied, and a week later we returned to Paris. There we spent another week trying to keep going before we flew home to Denmark, where I was placed in hospital with the diagnosis: a neglected concussion.

While all this was taking place, Karen Blixen had also been in hospital, although for more serious reasons. The exaggerated, euphoric mental receptivity that sometimes accompanies a depression of the sort that I suffered from had put me in a kind of telepathic communication with her. The first night, in the room facing the sea at the hotel in Brittany, I had heard her call out forcefully to me in the middle of a confused dream about my family. I had jumped out of bed and sat for a long time listening in the darkness as if her call had been real. I feared that something had happened to her, but I heard only the roar of the rising waves. The next day I wrote to her and asked if her call had meant that I should come home. I asked her to let me know, since this was the meaning of our pact of friendship. Three days

* Morten Nielsen (1922–1944) was a lyric poet active in the Resistance during World War II. —Tr.

later a letter came from Clara Svendsen* that the Baroness was in hospital and that she sent her greetings and thanks for my letter: "She asks me to say that she will do what you ask her to do when the time is ripe. She asks me to add that the elements that are truly sensitive to the moon must live with that fact, or forgive it that it pulls them in with so strong a rhythm." After my return home, while I was still in hospital, Karen Blixen told me how it was with her call that night. It was quite different from what I had surmised. While she was being treated for her painful disease, she had thought much of me, and that very night in a feeling that the pact was something unbearable, a burden on her and a danger for me, for which she dared not take the responsibility, she had cast me out with all her strength, out of the pact and out of her life. "When I saw a few days later, with the arrival of your letter, that you had, so to speak, ricocheted," she said, "and that I had drawn you to me as with a call, instead of irrevocably casting you out, I decided that if the pact between us ever has to be canceled, you will be the one who will have to do it."

---

*Clara Svendsen, who changed her name in 1980 to Clara Selborn, was for twenty years Karen Blixen's secretary and later her literary executor. She is the author of *Notater om Karen Blixen* (Notes on Karen Blixen), an account of her years of service. —Tr.

AT RUNGSTEDLUND ໄພ ໄພ ໄພ ໄພ
ໄພ ໄພ ໄພ ໄພ ໄພ ໄພ PELLEGRINA

AND SO the journey I had barely begun and of which I had
expected so much ended in a hospital bed. In a strange
way I felt set back all the way, not just to the time before the
journey but further back, and I slipped into a fatalistic feeling of
resignation and defeat, which in itself might have had some
healing effect. Not sick and not well, but in friendly surroundings, I was reading and enjoying various visits. Karen Blixen
came and brought me an amulet that was supposed to have a
curative effect. She said that first and foremost I should drop all
thought of my interrupted journey and commit myself totally
to the situation at hand. I should regret nothing, just think that
it had to be this way and no other and that everything would
come out all right if only I was prepared to receive and to give.
"God will make all things right," she said and quoted in her
old-Copenhagen accent the last two stanzas of Brorson's hymn*
with its somber fervor:

> God will make all things right:
> He will take you by the hand
> when you begin to fall away.
> When you sink into despair
> with little solace anywhere,
> in the valley of adversity.
> God upon that somber scene
> will Himself then intervene.

*Hans Adolph Brorson (1694–1764), a bishop and the most important
hymnist in Denmark during the Pietistic Movement of the eighteenth century. —Tr.

Then your grief will disappear
like a straw by fire consumed.

God will make all things right:
He by whose majestic might
the fearful dragon has been slain!
Although He may lead humankind
through excruciating pain,
wondrously at times.
Be prepared
for war and peace,
be prepared to give and take;
God will make all things right.

"Yes," she said, "these verses have helped me when everything was at its worst and I understood nothing. All that now
saddens you will one day vanish 'like a straw by fire consumed.'
Can you think of a better image for something disappearing?
And note the word *wondrously*. I have often thought of how I
have been led through excruciating pain *wondrously at times*."
She repeated these final words, drawing out each syllable.

The next time she came to see me, she repeated an invitation,
already extended through my wife, to come to Rungstedlund
after my release and stay with her there to regain my health in
isolation and peace. "There are three things I do well: tell
stories, cook, and look after mad people." She insisted, therefore, with particular respect to the latter, that she felt especially
called on to take care of me and make me well. "I shall lie like
a lioness on the threshold and guard against anyone's gaining
access to disturb you." In my immediate situation nothing
suited me better and I accepted with joy. Near the end of
September, I moved into the wing of the house at Rungstedlund
with the green room facing west and an adjacent bedroom.
Normally this was Karen Blixen's winter quarters, when the
fierce east wind blew through cracks and crevices in the east

wing and drove her out of Ewald's* room where she worked and from the bedroom above it.

In the beginning she had me eat alone, and in the course of a day we would be together at most an hour before I retired. Bedtime was fixed at nine P.M. by my severe keeper during my stay, which lasted until two days before Christmas. She would interrupt even the most exciting conversation often in the middle of a sentence when the grandfather clock struck nine. She would then get up and say, "Well, good night, Magister."

Karen Blixen came into the green room at about eight o'clock on the first evening. She sat down across from me and explained thoroughly and at great length the regimen she had in mind for me. She concluded by saying: "Would you consider settling down here with the feeling that your stay is indefinite, as it sometimes was for guests on the old Russian estates? They might stay for a month, but it also happened that they stayed for ten years. That is the way you should feel about it, while you are here, and spend no thought on time." And then she rose and placed a record on the old phonograph, given to her in Africa by Denys Finch-Hatton. But before putting the needle in the groove, she said slowly, "Just listen to the music, think of nothing else. You will hear this piece several times while you are here. The strains will wrap you up and rock your heart to rest in such a way that when you hear it again later in life, you will always remember these evenings and this green room where you first heard it." It was the adagio of Tschaikovsky's first string quartet, and I felt quite overwhelmed, receptive, and completely given over to the situation, taken away from all uncertainties that normally plagued me and from the disappointment of the interrupted stay in France to a remarkable dreamlike and

---

*Johannes Ewald (1743–1781), the greatest Danish lyric poet of the eighteenth century. From 1773 to 1775 he lived at Rungsted Kro, which later became Rungstedlund. He appears as a character in Isak Dinesen's story "Converse at Night in Copenhagen." —Tr.

yet wide-awake security. Karen Blixen sat there and gazed out into the September dusk and, once in a while, with kindness and penetration, at her guest. When the music was over, she got up, stopped the phonograph, said good night; and I went to bed with a profound feeling of homecoming.

I was consistently regarded as a convalescent and spoiled beyond measure. I was served breakfast in bed and otherwise left alone to read, take walks to the harbor, in the grove, over the fields and into the woods, and to listen to records. I might not even see the Baroness—she was always addressed in the third person as *baronessen*—for days on end. I would see no one at all but the housekeeper Mrs. Carlsen, who energetically and quietly took care of my meals. It was an odd feeling to be so alone in a large house, perceptibly alive all around me, seeing hardly anyone. The solitude undoubtedly was an important part of the cure, but at first it seemed to some extent empty and strange, an unexpected rebound after the marvelous and surprising familiarity of the first night. Urged by Karen Blixen, I kept a diary at the beginning of my stay until I began to write poems and to see her more often. On September 8, I made this entry:

Today was wonderful: everything has turned around. Hope, powerful and wonderful, has returned. I went for a walk in a steady mild drizzle that went through the soul as through an open door. The moon is almost full above Øresund; the Baroness called me to come out and look at it. The wind blows steadily in the trees and the sweet smell of fall comes in through the open window. I have in no way deserved this, but is it not often precisely what is undeserved that brings us the greatest joy? I rarely see the Baroness and until now we have talked only a bit. That is her will—that I be spared to the point of boredom. I feel her strong spirit everywhere; when I am weak, as a burden, unbearable; when I am

strong, as a liberation, like strong wings. Everything
around me takes place with a cheerfulness, regularity,
and calmness that makes me forget the surroundings
and makes me feel completely at home.

Yesterday she spoke briefly of Kenya. The impossible
conditions there have been mentioned lately in the
newspapers. B. told how she had written to Baldwin,
who had answered kindly but negatively, and how she
had tried to influence the Prince of Wales: "But Mrs.
Simpson ruined everything. All things considered, I
often feel that we have failed the natives. And look—
what I predicted at that time has now come to pass
exactly as I said it would. But no one would listen to
me. The Governor once asked me who could bring
order to this country, and I answered: 'I can.'" B. fell
silent for a moment and then added: "I should never
have come back home and written those books. I should
have stayed down there, it would have been much
better."

This regret was expressed with a seriousness and
sorrow that shocked me. It was incomprehensible to me
that this strong and competent person should so totally
reject the present period of her life and the books I
loved and regarded as the essence of her life's work. And
at the same time there was something perversely divine
about this gesture of rejection that made the deepest
impression on me; it made her grow and also become
humanly more intimate. There was a contradiction in
it that I could not resolve.

She took up this theme in other ways. A short while
later we spoke of her story "The Dreamers." Now that I
had come to know her, it had become clear to me and I
said so to her, "You are Pellegrina." And she answered,
"Yes, I am," and she added, "The loss of her voice

corresponds to my loss of the farm and Africa." Next
she expounded how it came to mean that she had lost
her destiny and her identity and that from that time
on she *willed* not to have a destiny, *willed* not to suffer
under any identity. In turn I told her of the tremendous
impact the tale had had on me when I read it for the
first time at the age of twenty, of the marvelous, mad
power of longing I felt flowing through it. Karen
Blixen replied that this story precisely, and for that
matter the whole book, was so powerful because it was
the first she had written after she lost the farm and
returned to Denmark. "It is like a scream, a lion's
roar," she said. "I could not write *Out of Africa* before
the pain abated."

Karen Blixen was quite interested in *Heretica* and contributed "Letters from a Land at War" to its first issue in 1948 and
"Converse at Night in Copenhagen" to its last issue in 1953.
Heretica had filled her with great expectations, which she felt
had been largely unmet. She would criticize the magazine from
one end to the other in a somber plaintive voice and foretell
ominously the course of events that she disapproved of wholeheartedly. Because the editors and the publisher had come to
consult her in the beginning, she thought the magazine some-
how had to be related to her view of life, which was of a pagan-
cosmic kind drawing on old traditions in which concepts such as
honor and destiny were integrated as a matter of course. She
found too little of this in *Heretica* and deplored its evangelical
Christian attitude and its philosophy of the brotherhood of man
and the ample apocalyptic talk about cultural crises. She found
the modern writers, with few exceptions, too squeamish, fussy,
and cheerless. Some of this feeling she got out of her system the
following evening when she came into the green room. After
speaking of her friend Denys Finch-Hatton, she said:

"Modern poets are not free spirits. Everything for them is painful. It is as if nothing can help them—just think of Rimbaud's terrible fate. Sometimes I'm accused of having only friends with good physiques. And that is perhaps correct. Denys Finch-Hatton was very handsome and had a perfect physique. He would never have wondered what anyone thought of him. It would never have occurred to him. The new poets want to be looked at, but when one looks at them they shout, No, no. Even Hans Christian Andersen, who was so unhappy and complained so much, could be made glad whenever he was a guest on some large estate or was acknowledged when he traveled about Europe. It was as if he only needed room to stretch his long legs. And Ewald was a free spirit; even in the depth of his degradation he often felt himself, with an overwhelming intensity, to be the darling of the gods."

Much of what Karen Blixen said about anything and everything was more or less openly addressed to me. In everything she continued to educate and encourage me, and urge me on. She did not hide that she expected the unusual of me, both humanly and poetically, and that could be most exciting, but also it could have the opposite effect since it was a task I felt to be far above my ability. Sometimes she amused herself making anagrams from people's names. She made one from Jørgen Gustava Brandt,* correctly using exactly the letters that comprise the name: *Antag vi er Guds Børn* (Assume we are God's children). From the name of Martin A. Hansen, whom she both admired and detested, she made: *Han er min Satan* (He is my Satan). One evening she wanted to air some sort of retrospective dissatisfaction with me. She had enough built up in her to do it in a predominantly positive fashion with an undertow of grim humor. She said:

*Jørgen Gustava Brandt (1929–   ), lyric poet and essayist, a painter, flaneur, and dandy, translator of Henry Miller and Dylan Thomas. —Tr.

"Now I will tell you something. Sometimes I think that you have been steeped in your environment like a biscuit dipped in a cup of coffee until it can be chewed without effort. I wish I'd been able to say to you: be hard. There is nothing wrong with soft bread, soft blankets, soft turf. But only hard things ring.

"I have made an anagram from your name: *Vridbor! Kling højt!* (Gimlet! Ring loud!) To make an anagram is more difficult than you think. Try it and see. This one could have been better, but it is not too bad either and I ponder it once in a while when I think of you. It would be nice to have a powerful, purposeful tool that rings loud and clear. A string on a violin is also hard, so is a bowstring, also a rather thin crystal glass can ring if it was hard enough to stand the grinding. And do become iron! Then you will feel what the biscuit never gets to feel, the power of the magnet going through you so that you become one with it. The biscuit may well maintain that the magnetic power is a beautiful illusion, that it is matched by no reality, and it may be difficult to argue with it. But the *steel* knows."

Thus she was on the one hand an unbending and teasing governess, and on the other, after the pact was made, completely open in a kind of thoughtful, friendly confidence. She fully displayed both sides during the months I stayed at Rungstedlund, and she now began to visit me more often in the green room.

On the evening of October third we had our first really extended conversation. From Byron and Shelley we came to discuss, among other things, our positions on Christianity, and I reported on the fluctuations in my own attitude toward it. Karen Blixen answered, "Yes, I have always felt that you young people are so troubled, that you have such a hard time finding out about such things. You are thrown into such doubt. I never doubt. I believe in God in the same way I always did." Later she went into the effect that never having attended school had had on her; her lack of schooling had perhaps made for greater continuity in her life. That was very interesting to me; and I told her about my time in school from my eighth to my fifteenth year, on the whole a period of suffering that carried with it a degradation and psychical diminution from which I then thought I should never recover. But now it felt remote and unbelievable and I never thought about it, although it undoubtedly had constituted a fatal break in the continuity of my life, in my natural development from youth to man. She thought it over for a long time and answered:

"The more I hear about your life, the more it confirms my understanding of you. I nod to myself and say, All right. Now I know the expression I was looking for the other day when we talked about those poets I called free spirits. It is this: that they are without bitterness, that they do not feel aggrieved as do almost all poets today. It is well that that period of your life has not sown bitterness in you, that you have forgotten it. That is why I feel so certain you will come through. Yes, I think I know what your life will become; but that I will not tell you now. You will become happy. Not that you will escape all unpleasantness and that everything will go smoothly for you; you will probably experience horrible things, and you may run into much adversity. But you will be happy."

She spoke finally of the longing one should never abandon: "I have always felt a mighty longing, even when it has not been realized. How can we long for something that does not exist? The migratory birds that are about to leave know they will set course for a land that exists." And she concluded with the wonderful words: "The longing itself is a pledge that what we long for exists!" In my diary, the notes on this evening end: "When B. speaks about these things she looks so beautiful, so eternally young." And my notes continue the next day: "This morning when B. came down, she said to me, 'I've got it. You are Peter in "Peter and Rosa."'" And that is the end of the diary, partly because I did not really care to keep it, partly because all my time from then on was divided between writing poetry and being together with Karen Blixen, either for afternoon walks in the Folehave woods or for evening conversations.

From Farah to Telemachos to biscuit to gimlet to Peter in "Peter and Rosa"—this was but the introduction to the metamorphoses I went through in Karen Blixen's consciousness, probably as taxing and exciting for her as they were for me. Sometimes she would be furious with me for reasons I could not fathom, and her vehemence was utterly incomprehensible. One evening, during an eruption of this kind, she literally shrank into a small, long-armed, gesticulating fury and left me, crushed and totally rejected, on the stroke of nine. I went to bed in a condition of numbness, unable to understand anything whatever. After a while the door opened and Karen Blixen slipped in and quietly sat down on the edge of my bed. But now she looked completely transformed, radiantly young and with a clear fullness to her features and with the erect slender grace of a seventeen-year-old, incomprehensible after the embittered net of wrinkles of a short while before. If I had not personally witnessed the transformation, I would not have believed it possible. And with a melodious floating tenderness in her voice she asked forgiveness for her outburst. She then went into the next room, left the door open, and played an *andante cantabile*, part of a string quartet by Haydn. On another occasion, when she came home from a visit to her cousin Count Bernstorff-Gyldensteen on Funen, she walked about stimulated and cheerful, straightening up things around the house, and in a terrible deep voice she sang verses from a hymn which she, with the substitution of "I" for "you," had introduced me to once when she felt I had suffered a gross injustice: "Who dares to curse when I would bless." These words were a vibration of magic security that went to my marrow. I was truly protected.

I began to see other inhabitants of the house. Old Petersen, the Baroness's chauffeur and handyman, glowered at me in an aloof but polite way, as at an unwelcome intruder. He would bring wood in for the stove only when I was out of the room. Once, long before, I promised Karen Blixen that I would carve our initials in the large tree at one end of the house. I shall always remember not just the expression on his face but his whole attitude of intense disapproval. He stood immobile and stared sullenly and menacingly while I whittled away and sweated profusely and did not quite feel I could explain that it was his mistress's own wish and that deep down I found it just as silly as he did. It belonged to the category of whimsical ideas she excelled in, which I hated to carry out. These are indeed the only initials I have carved in my life and the tree has now been cut down. On the evening when Karen Blixen went out to check that the letters had been properly carved and to give her approval of them, I told her of old Petersen's reaction. She enjoyed it heartily and said, "I know him. I can just see him; when something does not suit him and he can't stand it, he looks like the tall stump of an alder and emanates an eerie light like old touchwood." And there was Mrs. Carlsen, who managed the practical matters in the house with an energetic cheerfulness and who lamented loudly when I was late for meals, not the least so when it meant a sadly collapsed *gratin*. I disliked this particular dish and was more often late for it than for any other. In the end the idea formed in my head that *if* I was late, I would get the *gratin*—as some sort of mystical punishment. And so I began to hurry in order to avoid this awful dish. Although on several occasions she had strongly doubted my intelligence, not just in matters pertaining to her *gratin* although her doubts may have started with that, she was the only member of the household who was not influenced by the variations of her mistress's disposition toward me. Whether I was in or out of favor, she would receive me imperturbably in a friendly and cheerful manner, which later in critical situations would give me a soothing feeling that everything was as it used to be and that heaven and earth had not yet been disturbed. And I saw Mrs. Carlsen's little son who frolicked about like a son of the entire house. The Baroness read fairy tales to him in the evening in a deep, slightly nasal voice without dramatizing or accentuating a single event or line, but with long, slow waves of intonation. These were like the heavy swells after a storm raising and lowering the materials of the tale. It was a storyteller's reading, remarkable and fascinating.

And then there was Clara Svendsen, the secretary, with whom I discussed Byron, her favorite poet, and whom Karen Blixen did not always manage with ease, not because she was rash but because of a certain stubbornness in her nature. One evening, for example, when Clara insisted on playing one record more than the Baroness wanted to hear, the latter said jokingly in desperation, "It takes the strength of an elephant to control Clara," to which Clara replied, "Perhaps that is why the Baroness does not get anything else done." Once when the Baroness had entertained me for an entire afternoon while I was in bed with influenza, Clara came bursting in. The Baroness said: "Now that I've ordered Clara not to disturb you, she will probably say (and she broke into German), *'Sitzt nicht hier das lose Ding und tantaliert mit dem sterbenden Gnade'* (And yet, your grace, that loose woman sits there for hours flirting with the dying man)."

Another time when the Baroness was lunching with Clara and me, she said suddenly, "To think that I must content myself with you two for company! When I think of the people I have frequented in my lifetime, the magnificent Masais, General von Lettow and the Prince of Wales, Albert Schweitzer and Denys, Rothschild, Sir Laurence Olivier, and . . ." And here she dropped a few other glorious names and concluded, "And just to think that I have to sit here and make do with you." I understood her fully and did not feel that there was any answer. After an extended pause, during which the Baroness nibbled a bit of food and thoughtfully looked out the window as if we were air, she resumed her teasing from another direction and I could hardly get any food down for laughing.

Finally, and not to be forgotten, there was Pasop, Karen Blixen's German shepherd, of a tough, merry, and straightforward nature, who in her consciousness occupied a place neither inferior to nor less important than the one that Clara and I did. The Baroness was pleased that I like to spend much time with him outdoors, and my good relationship with him was in her eyes clearly a guarantee that, against all odds, even when I was at my worst, I was not completely lost.

While I was at Rungstedlund, my wife and friends would come now and then to see me, but their visits were rare and brief, as if limited to visiting hours. But once, my wife came over for the evening. Mrs. Carlsen prepared a magnificent meal of pheasant and red wine, served in the green room, while the Baroness was visiting a good friend nearby. We were alone and moved in a mood of elegiac rapture, enjoying being together and having such a splendid meal. We gave ourselves fully to the mood and to each other. But on the stroke of nine the Baroness returned, flung open the door, and sailed in like an ill-tempered swan that feels its brood threatened, bluntly declaring that my wife should go home and that I should go to bed.

There were no limits to the freedom Karen Blixen granted me or to the sovereignty she wanted me to exercise, unless I suddenly showed resistance to something she wanted me to do, something that I found unreasonable but not necessarily difficult, such as carving letters in a tree or escorting her to a certain embassy. She would then stamp her foot and hiss at me, "I can feel the white heat of your cowardice!" As long as just such trifles were concerned, I paid little attention. I always thought that one's courage should stand its test on more serious matters. And I did not yet understand that she could become so excited.

When she had shouted and been particularly harsh with me, she would then change key abruptly, come to sit down beside me, relaxed and intimate. With her most beautiful expression that bordered on transfiguration, she would say, "You must remember that deep down this is not at all what I meant to say. You must think of Sophus Claussen's* words about the Divine Serpent, 'When in its slough, venomous and murderous, it snorted, "It is all love."' Listen to the magnificent poet." Then she continued, quoting by heart a section of Claussen's poem "Man," and it was obvious that she, with a humorous and triumphant rapture all her own, identified herself with the serpent and life's dragon in the poem:

I often dare, when nights are inky black, to call on the
loveliness that dwells near the gates of death.

And in the sweet siesta hours, when the serpent was charmed
by its own big heart, I was chosen for lover.

Then it is imperative to seize the given moment to embrace
life's dragon that seeks my life.

But I must rest my hand on the world's steady axis to escape
the beast's revenge and its terrible claws.

I love the dragon's ferocity; serpents strike only those who
look upon them with poisoned eyes.

She looked harshly and challengingly at me for a long while until my head began to spin and I felt the desire for some vague but total submission.

*Sophus Claussen (1865–1931), considered one of the greatest modern Danish lyric poets. He lived for some time in Paris, where he became acquainted with the French Symbolist poets. Karen Blixen called his poetry her "Bible." —Tr.

AT RUNGSTEDLUND ✒ ✒ ✒ ✒
✒ ✒ ✒ ✒ THE DEVIL'S FRIEND

THIS was a perfectly happy time, and whatever happened was the result of love, pure love, and it irradiated me X-ray-like, healing, and yet with a mild clarity like that of the late October sun. I experienced the steady, complete joy of homecoming and a confirmation of what I had always believed, but had never put into words: "The longing itself is a pledge that what we long for exists." Now these words fell right into the chaos of a long poem I had planned and worked on for quite some time without success. It was a balm and a powerful antidote to the European Romantic tradition that saturated so much of the significant poetry I had lived with and so many bitter and difficult moments in my life. This Romantic tradition has been expressed, for example, in this line of Panthea's in Hölderlin's "Empedokles," which is taken so often out of context:

> Oh, eternal secret, what we are
> and seek we cannot find; what
> we find, we are not—

or this exclamation from Pär Lagerkvist's *The Vanquished Life* (*Det besegrade livet*)*: "Nothing satisfies the soul's longing. Not the sorrow, nor the profoundest joy. Because to be human is to hunger. Only hunger, hunger—for something that *does not exist*."

With all her human and poetic authority, like a veritable

---

* Pär Lagerkvist (1891–1974), Swedish Expressionist, lyric poet, novelist, and playwright; recipient of the Nobel Prize in 1951. *The Vanquished Life* is a collection of meditations and aphorisms marked by fervent idealism. —Tr.

guru, Karen Blixen had now told me *that it did exist* and had told me in such enchanted and natural words that it totally confirmed and fused with what had been until then my unconscious, but almost fundamental perception of life. The result of all this, the isolation and the protection I lived under, and the high, mild, and gentle October that wafted in from the Sound and through the woods, was that I finished the poem in some ten days in one blissful movement, a kind of continuous contemplation, which I experienced like the calm in the eye of the hurricane of feelings. It is one of my happiest poems, "The House of Childhood" (*Barndommens hus*), in which joy is not encapsulated in pain but rather in which pain is encapsulated in one great lasting joy. The poem is a definitive expression of fulfillment and homecoming. I found myself in a vast magnetic field of remembrance where I was not drawn down by the past, neither by the Atlantic coast of Brittany and my first experience there of the tremendous tide, all that recently had been interrupted for me, nor by my childhood home and the cloud-whales of my dreams on the Bay of Aarhus, but where the past, in almost euphoric delight, had been elevated to actuality in my adult life. It had grown with me into a kind of mythical durable structure, which was the breach and the period of emptiness between my eighth and fifteenth year filled up and healed, as I had said to Karen Blixen. From her words about longing, I could in triumphant affirmation and gratitude conclude the poem:

> The house is rebuilt: the heart's lofty
> articulation against doubt and disdain;
> somewhere under the sun and moon the wildest
> yearning in wonder finds its response.

These were happy times; I slept soundly and dreamt much and vividly and was completely cured of a chronic and painful insomnia caused by the concussion. When the writing of poetry is going well, I sometimes dream of verses that are either fully valid, or, in any case, essential cues when I awake. It is not at all as when the gold in the fairy tale's enchanted cave turns out to be withered leaves when exposed outside to broad daylight, as so often happens. While I was working on "The House of Childhood" and had reached the point I essentially regarded as the conclusion of the third section, I dreamt one night that I was together with the Baroness, who radiated confidence and wisdom and looked fantastically beautiful, not with the beauty of a seventeen-year-old, but with the beauty of her own age, and I talked enthusiastically to her about her confidence as a mighty, encouraging and inspiring example. In my dream I had shouted what is repeated almost verbatim in the last stanza of the third section of the poem: "Yes, yes, yes there is

> a confidence, deep as the roots of the mountains,
> which yet, in the shadow of age, will catch
> the last swallow, and with its slender
> sickle-shaped wing reap immortal happiness.

Like most writers who are engaged in something in earnest, I did not speak about what I was working on. At this time a young niece of Karen Blixen's was dying,* and was in an iron lung, if my memory is correct. From each visit to the patient, Karen Blixen came home deeply moved and told me about the young girl's condition and made me feel that it was far worthier of poetic effort than all the abstract charity and fellow-human-being philosophizing that occupied most contemporary poets. I took the hint and tried, but because I had never seen the young girl, the subject was too abstract for me in more than one respect. Because nothing came of it and I said nothing of what all I was doing, my silence created in the Baroness a disappoint-

---

* Karen de Neergaard Sveinbjørnsson, who had contracted meningitis at the immunization hospital in Copenhagen, where she worked. —Tr.

ment of the kind that could turn into one of her—to me incomprehensible—outbursts of rage, but in this case did not.
Ecstatically I kept working on the long poem.

One evening in November, when I was sure we would not be
disturbed, I read the new poem aloud to her, wanting her to
judge not the worth of the poem as such but what it was worth
between us in terms of our pact. My reading took place in the
green room, and when I had finished there followed a long,
dizzying silence that rang in my ears like a delicate treble, of the
sort that may occur in a state of high intoxication. I have known
no one, ever, who was such a master as Karen Blixen of long
periods of silence, not the embarrassed, offended, or confused
kind, but the active, open kind. After the long silence she
slowly rose, walked over to me, put her hand around the back of
my head and kissed me on my forehead, whereupon she returned to her chair and sat down again. She had the answer now
and the long silence that followed was bearable. Then she began
to speak, saying that this was what she had hoped for but had
not expected. Now she knew that she had been right. Some very
simple and clear remarks about the poem followed and then one
sharp rebuke because, in the heat of composition, I had mistaken a waning morning moon for a new moon, which cannot
occur in the eastern morning sky. She said that no matter how
imaginatively I wrote, I had to show as much exactness in my
poetry as an astronomer in his journal or as a hunter or a sailor
who had knowledge of these matters. After a heartfelt lecture on
the general state of ignorance these days of the nature, movement, and changing appearance of the heavenly bodies and in
particular on my unforgivable lack of knowledge, she fell silent
again. The lecture later resulted in my study of astronomy.
Then she began to tease me.

"You have really fooled me lately," she said. "It is as in the
tale of Hansel and Gretel. Here I have kept you securely locked
up and every time I have come to see if you have gained weight

and become fat enough for a feast, like Hansel you have stuck a gnawed bone out between the bars instead of your finger. Now I can finally feel how fit and plump you have become." Just then the clock struck nine.

About this time she gave me her essay on H. C. Branner's *The Riding Master* to read. She was exasperated in this essay over the confusion of myth and mystery. She felt herself to be unmistakably one with Hubert, the Centaur, who lived entirely in myth, who laughed at the perils that others felt, who laughed in general: the Centaur whom the others felt to be both attractive and frightening, indispensable in life and yet one they would have preferred to see dead. When Karen Blixen met reproach or denunciation, often of a kind many would have ignored, she would bitterly and mournfully say over and over: "*May* I not exist? May I not be permitted to exist at all?" No more than Hubert was allowed to exist, she felt. And here came the others, thinking that they could revive and strengthen the anemic and dying mystery, the mystery of the love of one's fellow man, by a blood transfusion from the myth, from the hard and innocent animality, by nourishment from the primeval which they simultaneously denied, wanted no part of—or wanted to falsify, humanize, render impotent. She thought that a compassionate savior mania like that of Clemens in *The Riding Master* was a debasement, a decomposition, and a weakening of those to whom it was applied. Only he who truly was glad himself would really be able to make others glad. Therefore, in the essay she had especially noted these lines from my poem "The House of Childhood": "and I am a riddle to myself and stand unmoved as a herald of gladness." Karen Blixen scrupulously asked me if I had any objection to this use of my words, and I could only say truthfully that I was proud of it.

Just as Karen Blixen acknowledged in herself Hubert's centaurlike hardness, so she also professed victory and wanted me to do the same. In *Letters from a Land at War* she became apprehensive about the fanatical and triumphal will to victory that she sensed during her visit to the Third Reich, heard there through the spirit—or lack of spirit—in a performance of Beethoven's Fifth Symphony. But that was because it was the titanic victory of endured suffering, a victory without real joy. It was a different kind of victory that she referred to when, in the encouraging letter she had sent to me in Paris, she had said: "The very day you receive this letter, go to the Louvre and look at the Victory of Samothrace." She felt that suffering and defeat, loss and weakness had been made into a kind of metaphysics that she deplored and found totally unacceptable. Early in our acquaintance her abhorrence of this attitude to life was pointedly expressed in a letter she sent me together with Eyvind Johnson's rewriting of *The Odyssey*:*

> Herewith Eyvind Johnson's book that I told you about.
> I know you are very busy, so I am not asking you to
> read all of it. But if you could manage to read the last
> two chapters you might explain to me why the same
> events at one time became *The Odyssey*, and now, for
> Eyvind Johnson, have spawned this book. Though I
> cannot claim to belong to Homer's generation, I feel
> that I and the persons, black or white, whom I have
> been associated with in my life have more in common
> with it than we can possibly have with a generation that
> will not acknowledge victory, but turns away from it
> and denies it. Is it not ultimately sensible and decent
> to wish defeat for the people who really love defeat,
> who must have it and for whom it is far less bitter and
> painful than victory?

* *Surf Against the Shores, A Novel About the Present (Strändernas Svall)* by Eyvind Johnson, Swedish novelist who shared the Nobel Prize in 1974 with Harry Martinson. —Tr.

Karen Blixen also took great pleasure in acknowledging a kinship with the Devil, who gives one victory and power over everything in this world for passion and plunder, if one promises him one's soul in return. For specific reasons he had, however, given her something else. She told me this one evening in December when she returned to the subject of the disease that had separated her from life, first and foremost the sexual part of it, at an early age: "When that happened to me and there was no help to be had from God, and you should be able to understand how terrible it is for a young woman to be denied the right to love, I promised the Devil my soul and he promised me in return that everything I experienced thereafter would become a story. As you can see, he has kept his promise." We were sitting before the fireplace and for a long time after the final words she gazed mournfully into the fire, and the silence grew as if nothing existed but silence and the barely audible flames. What she had just told me sounded like the truth, a decisive truth regardless of the strange and unlikely framework it had been given. On the other hand, I could not take her quite seriously when she, almost without transition and using the same imagery, would suddenly interject into a conversation: "Wouldn't you like to meet my good friend? Yes, my best friend, the Devil." Such statements she stubbornly repeated and sometimes enlarged upon: "Won't you get up on the broomstick with me?" I was usually taken by surprise and, bewildered, did not know how to answer. I thought a "yes" and a "no" equally impossible, and because more specific instructions did not follow on how one or the other should be carried out, nothing happened. Calmly and deliberately the Baroness resumed the conversation as if her suggestions had never been made.

The days passed and everything about me ran its course as if I were to stay on indefinitely. To Karen Blixen's great displeasure, I not only had friends outside Rungstedlund, but also and worst of all, had a family, a wife and a child. She did what she could to accept this, but she ascribed the failure of my stay in France, among other things, to the presence of my three-year-old son during the last part of it, and her annoyance could, with studied sarcasm, break through in a remark such as: "So you thought you could go out and seek the holy grail with a perambulator, did you?" It was decided all the same that I should celebrate Christmas with my family while Karen Blixen went to visit her feudal friends on Funen.* The night before Christmas Eve was celebrated with all the inhabitants of the house. It was a lovely light-headed evening, during which Karen Blixen ingeniously participated in all kinds of fun and games with her enigmatic smile. She laughed generously, as it befitted a demi-goddess and friend of the Devil plunging incognito into a saturnalia. The next morning I went home to my family. I had stayed then at Rungstedlund for exactly three months, and the lioness, which the Baroness also was, had indeed guarded me and made me well.

---

*Inger and Julius Wedell at Wedellsborg, their estate on Funen. —Tr.

CONVERSATIONS ❧ ❧ ❧ ❧ ❧

L IKE no one I had ever met, Karen Blixen played herself out in two vastly different forms of conversation. The one that would regularly take place when several people with whom she was only slightly acquainted were present was pure conversation, full of stereotyped phrases conditioned by her background, totally unaffected by the possible repetitions of what she had said hundreds of times and regardless of whether there were persons present who knew already what she was saying backward and forward. It was a veritable show, a circus ride through tried witticisms and paradoxes, anecdotes and old tales. With age anyone may chance to repeat himself—usually unwillingly and unawares—but here it seemed deliberate, as if she were completely indifferent to the matter. People would have to put up with it if she had to put up with them. Sometimes she seemed to prefer to be bored by her own repetitions (which, after all, were of her world and might say something to others) rather than by other peoples' trivialities. She would often talk inconsiderately over their heads and with hardly a pause. I was fascinated in a very special way by this form of conversation, taking in only the person and hardly at all what was said; sometimes it seemed almost shameless and pathetic when I thought of what she also *could* say—of her other form of conversation. But at times I felt that I understood that there was some kind of protection in this manner and that this was what she meant by "grinning back at the Devil," which she also expected me to do in similar situations. But it was not in my nature to do so.

It is well known that there are two kinds of wit, one that consists in the recapitulation of funny situations, the retelling of jokes, anecdotes, and of all sorts of stories and the other that springs spontaneously from the situation at hand, brand new and never before expressed. Karen Blixen mastered both kinds to perfection, but it was the latter that characterized her second form of conversation. Not just the wit but everything connected with it was generated by the situation. Her conversation was therefore slow and attentive, concentrated and seemingly supervised by her large, intent, attentive eyes, and with many long pauses. She looked at times as if she knew everything (in a way she probably did) and as if it was possible to dispense this fullness only gradually in small amounts. And when she was faced with something insurmountable she limited herself to saying mysteriously: "I know it, I know it." I did not doubt her word. If the conversation had concerned one's undertakings and potentialities, she would appear sibylline, Norn-like, as if she were contemplating every aspect of one's life. But this ability could also find more detailed and concrete expression; indeed, in periods of close and intense contact, she not only knew what I had thought and felt while I had been elsewhere, she knew precisely where I had been and what I had done and she would tell me. Not just tell me but make what she told me a part of the conversation as if it were not at all out of the ordinary, or at least that it was in line with everything else on the subject that we were pursuing. Undoubtedly that was the way she felt about it while I sat there feeling slightly dizzy as after an electric shock. I was not only protected, but, it seemed to me, supervised in a supernatural way.

In these conversations, Karen Blixen to an unusual degree explained herself graphically, as far as possible avoiding concepts and abstractions, without replacing them excessively by similes, as is too often done. She could express herself with surprising simplicity about very complicated matters, as has probably always been the way of the wise, and, like the wise, she said things with a subtle, polite respect, and again with an undisguised contempt for learning and complexity, plain and profound at the same time. What she said was meant for immediate use in life and not for a textbook. In these conversations, born of situations, in this spoken intercourse there were moments when I found her wiser than in anything she had written. She might speak as if she had never written anything, while at other times she referred frequently to *Out of Africa* or to her tales. I relate comparatively little of these conversations because in general I remember but fragments of them. It is as with one's deep dreams and the profound books to which one must return again and again, and which are remembered only approximately and of which only the strongest impressions are recalled because ordinary life is by no means lived on that level; one is not wise all the time. As a rule I did not write down the conversations partly because, while they took place, I was confident that I would always remember them and partly because something in me protested against such a record, as if it would rob what was said of its profound comprehensive effect.

It was naturally demanding to be a partner in such conversations. Sometimes my strict partner would be happy and content; if she was not, I would be severely chastised, and on points on which I least expected to be, ones on which I had never before been rebuked simply because I had not grasped that there was anything about them deserving of reproof. Sometimes I would get a strong urge to laugh without external cause or provocation. It was like a groundless, inordinate, organic, and mental well-being that had to find an expression. I felt a huge bubble of laughter rise in me and quickly I would, often uncritically, haphazardly, say something funny in order that the laughter not seem completely unmotivated, and then I would laugh long and heartily. I had always envied the one who could tell jokes with an imperturbable poker face. That I could not do, as the Baroness had obviously seen. She easily took part in my laughing excesses; but one day when my guffaws must have seemed particularly unprovoked, she said disapprovingly and with dead seriousness: "Listen, Magister, when you feel such an unmanageable urge to enjoy yourself, it is your duty, indeed, you owe it to me, to say something truly funny, to give the rest of us reason to participate in the merriment when you get that notion to laugh at any cost. You must prevail upon yourself to make the effort to come up with something that we can laugh at also instead of being bored." Such a reproof I had neither expected nor ever been subjected to before; I became deeply embarrassed and since then have really made the effort in what has become a conditioned reflex, to say something that approximately corresponds to the inadvertently rising bubble of laughter. And it took some time before I dared to try being funny again, at least in her presence.

In our conversations, Karen Blixen did not accept poor memory. Here also she made unexpected demands on me. In a conversation about Denys Finch-Hatton, his nature, and his condition at the time Karen Blixen was preparing to leave Africa, a condition that may have contributed to his airplane crash and death (that never has been and probably never will be fully explained), I said that something in his condition reminded me of Goethe's poem *"Selige Sehnsucht"* (Ecstasy and Desire). She wanted to hear the poem, which she did not know, and I asked where she kept Goethe's works. She replied that she did not have them because she did not understand and did not read German. That was not true because she could recite at length in German entire passages of Heine, whom she loved and rated high above Goethe, the opposite of what I felt. "Your Goethe," she would say teasingly, "that *petit maître.*" There I sat, accustomed to look up what I could not remember but without any reference book to turn to. "Try really hard to remember it." I tried, but could not. Just then Clara Svendsen came to report a telephone call for the Baroness. She got up, gave me an irritated and harsh look and said: "When I come back, you will remember the poem." She was right. When she came back some minutes later, I could recite it.

Karen Blixen did not think aids should be refused when really needed, and when she wanted to she used reference books and dictionaries diligently; both Clara and I were repeatedly sent to fetch them for her. But she strongly felt that my generation had become addicted to the vice of convenience and in an unjustifiable and self-indulgent manner shunned difficulties that, by being surmounted, would give greater insight and experience. Early in our acquaintance this led me to write the following dedication to her in my edition of the works of Martin A. Hansen: "To K. B.—with thanks for the inspiring lesson—that it is essential to jump over the fence at its highest point." She was confused and rather hurt by this and did not find it funny at all. Did I, for example, believe she would advise someone to jump over a fence where it was highest if he was pursued by a snorting bull? Concerning the power of memory, she thought that the extensive use of books and the dependence on the printed word had dulled it and that it would be sharpened if one grew accustomed to trying to recall what was in a book rather than immediately reaching for it when something in it was needed. She said that generally we could remember much more than we thought we could and that in Africa she had lived among people whose memory had to function entirely without books. She herself had a fantastic memory and she could quote not only a stanza now and then, but very long poems without hesitation or uncertainty, whole passages from the Bible, the Koran, and the Homeric poems. Later I thought that it contributed to making our conversations so intense and coherent, so free of disturbing interruptions, not to have to take time to look things up in books. Her inflexible demand improved my memory and I was often astonished and impressed by what I was able to remember when really put to the test.

That Karen Blixen was acutely aware of the worth and dimension of this second form of conversation became clear from her preoccupation with the original form of such conversation, namely, the symposium. Today the word symposium is loosely used to designate debates and discussions meant to be something more than mere exchanges of stereotyped and finished opinions, but Karen Blixen always literally had in mind Plato's symposium, Plato's banquet. On the basis of a dream she had had, she sometimes tried to arrange gatherings of vastly different people at Rungstedlund—for example, on the subject of Christianity; but although such gatherings fascinated her, she was far from satisfied. As it happened, I never got to sit in on such a meeting, but I had the impression that she got more out of them when very few people were present, even only one other person. She enjoyed composing imaginary symposia. She would sit down, look at me full of expectation and say: "Now whom shall we invite if we imagine a symposium and can choose freely among all the living and the dead?" After I had pondered for a while, the long pause having for me become quite normal in these conversations, she said, "Well, I don't want any prophets, because one cannot converse with them. They only want to speak and not to listen; so they are no good for a symposium, however much they may mean to mankind. Moses, Mohammed, or Grundtvig* will therefore not be invited. But Goethe ought to be here; it must be delightful to talk with him and he will carefully listen to what others say." I was tremendously pleased thus to have my "*petit maître*" restored to favor. She also mentioned as possibilities Niels Bohr and Saint Francis of Assisi because she felt that the symposium should not consist of poets only and that we had to think of whether the persons under consideration had something to say to one another. That was also the way she planned real gatherings, but inasmuch as there

*N. F. S. Grundtvig (1783–1872), bishop, the most important Danish hymnist of modern times, founder of the Danish People's High School. —Tr.

were no limits I proposed Lao-Tzu and Li Po. This arrogant and extravagant party game, which was resumed at intervals, probably served mostly to crystallize concepts of certain human qualities, not the most outstanding and epoch-making, but the most immediately fascinating and psychically productive in intimate mental exchange. Definitely it had something to do with the kind of genius the Baroness represented, not the genius of the apostle (to use Kierkegaard's distinction), nor that of the sage, but one developed in human companionship to "a higher amiability." That is Eckersberg's* definition of art, which Karen Blixen loved to quote.

The symposium, the second form of conversation, set precisely in a festive, amiable, erotically accentuated atmosphere, thus served Karen Blixen as a means to deeper insights than men and women are usually granted. This is exactly as she describes it in "Converse at Night in Copenhagen," a carefully constructed symposium tale of an imagined meeting between Johannes Ewald and the insane King Christian the Seventh. Later I realized that she was working on this story at the time we discussed the nature of the symposium.

Karen Blixen had let me read in manuscript several tales from what later became *Anecdotes of Destiny* and *Last Tales* and asked for my critical assessment of them. When I stayed again at Rungstedlund the following year, in September 1951, while Karen Blixen was laid up sick at the other end of the house—we kept in touch by letters because she did not want visits—I was handed "Converse at Night in Copenhagen" with this note:

Dear Magister:

    After some hesitation, I am sending you "Converse at Night in Copenhagen," but not as a literary gift. The story does not move from author to author in order

---

*C. W. Eckersberg (1783–1853), painter and pupil of the French painter J. L. David, professor at the Academy of Art in Copenhagen. —Tr.

to attain a judgment of its descriptions of nature or the development of its ethical attitude. It goes to you because we are good friends, and I might just as well give you a bouquet of roses or a kiss.

When Karen Blixen became well enough for us to meet again for supper, we spoke, among other things, of the tale, which had delighted me, as if with the music of the spheres. The story was like a frank confidence, a long echo of glorious conversations, and the elucidation and consummation of recurring themes. She said there was something missing in it that she would like me to help her remedy. It concerned Ewald Yorick's last remark to the king that preferably should conclude metrically in the distinct rhythm of an ode, as in Ewald's "Ode to My Moltke" (*Ode til min Moltke*). Again and again she had tried without success, but she felt certain that I could do it, and after that she showed me the passage she had left open along with several drafts, so that I might fully understand what was supposed to be there. At last she said: "You may consider it this way: Aladdin has now let the genie erect the palace; but as a special favor and in order that you may realize that it is not just given to anyone to build such a palace, one window has been left incomplete so that you may realize how difficult it will be to finish it, but also that the building, once you have given it the finishing touch, will be quite grateful to you for its completion." After this playfully proud and pretended self-effacing courtesy to me and its appeal to my skill as a craftsman, I immediately tackled the problem, "the window," which was not solely of a metrical nature but required a highly developed rhythm and a very special choice of words. Thank God the storyteller was satisfied with the result; if not, I would have worked on the lines until she was. I have reason to believe that in my poem "The House of Childhood" as in "Converse at Night in Copenhagen" there is a reflection of the happiest and strongest moments of my relationship with Karen Blixen. It was ironic that we contributed this story and this poem to the final issue of the magazine *Heretica*, which ceased publication after six years.

At this time Kelvin Lindemann, under the pen name of Alexis Hareng, published *An Evening in the Cholera-Year, or The Red Umbrellas (En Aften i Kolera-Aaret)*.* The publisher announced its publication so cunningly and brazenly that one was led to believe that it was a new book by Karen Blixen, one like *The Angelic Avengers*, only with a new pseudonym. This was strongly hinted in a circular sent out to the bookstores under the heading "Strictly Confidential." Karen Blixen became angry and deeply upset by this affair, especially when she found out who the author really was, because she had often talked with him. "He was like a big friendly dog," she said, "that jumped up and put his paws on my shoulders and almost knocked me over." Now she felt that she had been betrayed and exploited. But her anger was first and foremost directed against the publishing house and its speculation in her name and her pseudonyms and against the reviewers who, with a few righteous exceptions, had written about the book and evaluated it as a work that could be hers. And she was furious with them whether they had praised the book or denounced it. She had turned in the manuscript of "Converse at Night in Copenhagen" to the editor of *Heretica* before all this happened, but now she wanted to withdraw it because she was deeply offended. She had declared that henceforth not a single word of hers would be published in Danish. I thought this was an unreasonable reaction. The editors asked me to persuade her to let the story be printed anyway, and since I was in the process of writing an article about the whole affair, I decided to make her see how

---

*Published in New York by Appleton-Century-Croft in 1955 as *The Red Umbrellas*. —Tr.

untenable her position was. When I attempted to reason with her, she said that she could see no reason why it had been believed that she was the author and why this deception had been undertaken in the first place. In any case, I said, this was not a reason for her discontinuing publication in Danish. After all, on one occasion when Mozart was asked how he would refute his detractors, reviewers, and derogatory critics, he said, "I do not hear them; I will refute them with my new works."

At last I asked her if, in spite of it all, she did not think there would be more common sense and superiority in such an attitude than in letting a whole nation pay for the excesses of a few culprits; if it would not be far better to continue and let "Converse at Night in Copenhagen" be printed in *Heretica* as a single irrefutable and glorious answer. When she bitterly answered "No," I teased her by saying that then I would demonstrate my perfect solidarity with her by withdrawing "The House of Childhood" from *Heretica* also, and, furthermore, that I would not publish anything in Danish before she did. This suggestion put her in a better mood and at last she thanked me for having mentioned Mozart's example. In the end both our contributions appeared in *Heretica*.

In those days, and particularly just after my stay at Rungstedlund, there was a tremendous friction in me between the certainty of what I wanted to do and the uncertainty of my means of realizing it. Karen Blixen had a keen eye precisely for this inner conflict, and time and time again she said both in conversation and in letters, as Jesus said to Martha, "You are worried and upset about many things, but only one thing is needed." Once while she was abroad, and my affairs had taken a turn for the better after a difficult period, she wrote, "When you make it clear to yourself with sufficient force that one thing only is required, everything will obey the order nicely; everything will stand at attention and await detailed instructions." It was true, at least for that situation, but by no means always. Karen

Blixen knew well the means it took to realize the one required thing in her world, but sometimes she had no idea whatever of what it took to realize it in my world. She would not recognize obstacles; she demanded that you at least should "throw your heart over the hurdle," as she put it, and it did help to remove or overcome many imagined hindrances. But she wanted to treat real and invincible obstacles the same way, mine and sometimes her own, and much trouble came of her doing so. Her genius allowed her at times to see through this with ease. Just as easily as she could see through one and know what the one thing required was for that person, so just as surely she could lament, "I know it will go wrong, no matter what I do to avoid it. Everything I undertake goes wrong. So it did when I brought one of my servants from Africa to this house and what I am doing with you will also go wrong. I *cannot* refrain from trying what cannot be done." Later she made light of it, but she was right. It did go wrong.

Thorkild Bjørnvig and Karen Blixen in 1950. Photo by Knud W. Jensen. Courtesy of the Royal Library of Copenhagen.

Photo by Holt-Madsen.

Courtesy of the Royal Danish Ministry for Foreign Affairs.

Rungstedlund about 1950. Photo by Johannes Overeng. Courtesy of the Royal Library of Copenhagen.

The drawing room at Rungstedlund. Photo by John Stewart. Courtesy of Parmenia Migel.

Karen Blixen with her Scots deerhounds in the garden of the Kenya farm in 1914. Courtesy of the Royal Danish Ministry for Foreign Affairs.

At work in "Ewald's Room," about 1956. Photo by Clara Svendsen. Courtesy of Parmenia Migel.

Karen Blixen and Albert Schweitzer during their meeting in Copenhagen in 1954. Photo by Tage Christensen. Courtesy of the Royal Library of Copenhagen.

With Marilyn Monroe and Carson McCullers, New York, 1959. Courtesy of the Royal Library of Copenhagen.

Dressed in the Pierrot costume. Photo by Rie Nissen, 1954. Courtesy of the Royal Library of Copenhagen.

Frank Jaeger, about 1951. Courtesy of the
Royal Library of Copenhagen.

H. C. Branner. Photo by Hans Robertson,
about 1949. Courtesy of the Royal Library of
Copenhagen.

Ole Wivel, 1948. Courtesy of the Royal Library
of Copenhagen.

Jørgen Gustava Brandt. Photo by Holt-Madsen, 1957. Courtesy of the Royal Library of Copenhagen.

Thorkild Bjørnvig

Photo by John Stewart. Courtesy of Parmenia Migel.

A SPRING OF INDECISION 🐦🐦🐦

K AREN BLIXEN and I had agreed that I should visit her
weekly or at least fortnightly after my return to my family. Sometimes I arrived in the afternoon if there was something
definite we were to discuss. One day it was "Daguerreotypes,"
about which she asked me to give my unreserved opinion,
which I did. She flew into a rage when I criticized a few points,
only to deliver her grateful approval of my "honest criticism"
and my "good judgment" on the next visit. Dinner was served
that time in the green room where I had worked for three
months. No one else was present; if anyone had been, we would
have dined in the other wing of the house. There we were, with
excellent food and a bottle of red wine. Karen Blixen drank only
a single glass to toast me slowly and ritually; I drank the rest.
She did not eat much either. But fully restored to health, I
enjoyed both food and drink. This time I was not put to bed at
nine o'clock. We had coffee after dinner, and I was presented
with a bottle of cognac shaped like a pig, which I took delight in
emptying.

On this occasion our conversation was without intent or
plan, rather like talk in a free-flowing and exuberant symposium. In my advanced state of intoxication I sometimes
talked like a waterfall and made statements, guided by some
magnetic perspicacity, that one normally must search the heart
and try the brain to formulate. Or I was suddenly interrupted by
an exhilaration that struck like bolts of lightning and dazzled
my entire being. Strangely enough, without drinking anything
but a little water and coffee, Karen Blixen literally went along
with my state of rapture; excited, attentive, laughing far more
frequently than she normally did, now and then gently tugging
my hair as she went by me to fetch or arrange something. While
I listened intently with my whole being, she said heartwarming

things or terrible ones, told stories and reminisced with the chorus from "Daguerreotypes:" "I am imagining, for one may imagine anything and everything." But what was imagined was more monstrous on this occasion.

On one such evening she told me for the first time about her marriage, which until then she had only touched on lightly, and described her husband in detail. She concluded by saying, "I have portrayed him precisely as he was in 'The Dreamers.' He could not bear to let me have anything all to myself. He only knew what he wanted after I knew what I wanted. Yes, he is Baron Gyldenstierne." Or she imagined what we would do when we went to see the Shakespeare plays performed at Stratford-on-Avon. She loved in general to fantasize about travel, but she could also have sudden, apparently unmotivated, fits of despair. After one of these she would play Schubert's songs from "The Winter Journey" (*Die Winterreise*), especially those from the final sections, "The Signpost" (*Der Wegweiser*), "The Mock Suns" (*Die Nebensonnen*), and "The Organ Grinder" (*Der Leiermann*), and listen as though in a deep transport of melancholy. When the record with *Der Wegweiser* finished, she would mutter to herself, "*Habe ja doch nichts begangen/Dass ich Menschen sollte scheu'n?*" (Have I after all done anything that would make me shun people?) And she would find herself in "The Organ Grinder" (*Der Leiermann*), that extreme expression of groundless abandonment, self-willed desolation and self-banishment to the periphery of existence, to some dismal wilderness, in such lines as:

> *Keiner mag ihn hören,*
> *keiner sieht ihn an,*
> *und die Hunde knurren*
> *um den alten Mann*

> (Nobody wants to hear him,
> nobody looks at him,
> and the dogs snarl
> at the old man)

and she would say, "Do you hear, can you see—there I am!" This also corresponded to her imagined identification with the deserted King Lear. But there were other pieces in her fascinating mosaic of quotations. She loved Uhland's and Schubert's "Faith in Spring" (*Frühlingsglaube*), and when she had listened to it she often nodded her hopeful assent and repeated the chorus, "Now everything must take a turn for the better" (*Nun muss sich alles, alles wenden*) as if in some mysterious way it was valid for her as well as for me and was what we were all about. "Don't you think '*Es blüht das fernste, tiefste Tal*' (the farthest, deepest valley is blooming) is a lovely line?" she asked on one of those evenings in early spring. Denys and I agreed that it was a certain valley we could see from the farm, the farthest and the deepest, just after the rainy season. Yes, sometimes when we are together I think it is like an echo of that time, frailer but the same, the same." And thus she swung between high expectation and the deepest despair.

When on such occasions I finally went to bed in the adjoining bedroom, she would remain seated in the green room and, when blissfully inebriated I lay tucked under the comforter, she would open the door and put a record on the gramophone. At times I would fall asleep while the music played, at others I heard her quietly remove the record, close the machine, and shut the door. The next morning I would usually go home without seeing her, but it did happen that I sometimes stayed for lunch, when normally others would be present. My existence had found its center of gravity and point of rest at Rungstedlund and Sletten, where I had my family and a study facing east behind the crown of a lime tree. I felt in all ways privileged and I committed myself completely to the writing of poetry.

At the beginning of 1951, the University of Copenhagen announced a grant for summer study at the University of Bonn, similar to the one I had received in Paris. It was suggested that I apply for it. Because I told Karen Blixen everything, I also mentioned this, but I had not thought of applying for it in any case because it ran counter to all my plans for that year. But Karen Blixen became quite excited about it and held that I must absolutely apply; this was an offer I could refuse with neither justification nor decency. It must be a sign from the powers that be that it came just at this moment. I did not feel anything of the kind and I was unable to share her enthusiasm for the project. But that she was so sure of it naturally impressed me; I became doubtful and said so. When I came to visit shortly thereafter, Karen Blixen put before me the following form:

RITUAL FOR A CHOICE

I . . . . make this decision in earnest, as an honest person.

I renounce and exclude any subsequent regret or doubt pertaining to my decision, inasmuch as I earnestly and honestly reject and refuse hereafter to return to the thought of an alternative.

So help me Goethe, Rilke, and Hölderlin.

I adhere to and retain in my consciousness, in earnestness and honesty, the certainty that my decision, in practice, is and remains of exceptionally little importance.

. . . . . . this . . . . 19 . . . . .

Karen Blixen was enough of a connoisseur of souls to know that the diagnosis in the form would impress itself upon me, but not enough of one to know that I would use the last clever phrase of it to make the decision that suited *me* and not her. Because I still found it completely meaningless to interrupt the course I was pursuing because of—in my *honest* opinion—a wholly incidental, extraneous occurrence and for something that fit in nowhere in that course, I decided once again not to apply and told her so. I did not sign the form. I had a feeling that that would transform it from a piece of wisdom which I, in spite of everything, unashamedly could fail to live up to into a charter I in decency could not break. But it now became clear that *she* could not stick to the precept that my decision in practice was "of exceptionally little importance." She was deeply disappointed and what she considered my incorrect decision generated a tension between us that took me by surprise. The Baroness obviously got into a conflict with herself because, on the one hand, she felt absolutely certain that I ought to go to Bonn and, on the other, she had to accept that I would not go no matter how incomprehensible it appeared to her. My idiotic refusal was like an offense and a contradiction, an inconceivable negation of her secret knowledge of me, to which she had to react. Shortly thereafter I received this letter, dated March 7, 1951:

Dear Magister:

Forgive me for this letter, and do not take it as a break in the conditions that we have set. I am absolutely certain that you have made your decision as an honest person guided by the most assured conviction. This I will always believe of you and I have furthermore promised, or given my word, that I will believe it; so there is no doubt in my mind. But I myself am weak, or my brain is a bit clouded—I cannot explain your decision to myself. I keep thinking that you would be able to explain it to me. But for you to begin to explain would really violate the conditions that we have set: never to return to the thought of an alternative.

Therefore, let us wait a bit before we see each other again. Perhaps I shall be inspired to find a way to understand. Or your work will itself give me the fullest explanation.

I wish everything good possible in this world for
your work—as for your total satisfaction with this
existence—which *cannot* be affected by my blindness!

I should have stuck to this last statement, and even at the risk
of endangering our relationship I should have stayed responsi-
bly on my course. But that I did not do. With the high tension
between us and the thought of our pact of friendship, I did not
have the nerve to bear the unmistakable disappointment and
disapproval implied in the letter in spite of all the assurances
that the letter also contained. Moreover, during a visit I stood
on Ewald's Hill and thought that the Norn or the Muse after all
had to know better than I and that it was foolish of me to resist.
Consequently, I changed my mind and applied. Karen Blixen
wrote to me in answer to my decision that she and Clara were
delighted and that they had played the "*Marseillaise*" on Denys
Finch-Hatton's old gramophone. But there was less cause
for celebration than she realized. I was glad, of course, because
she was glad but not because of the decision, however much I
might wish it. I still did not understand why it was so important to her and why it should be to me. I could only hope to
come to understand after it had been carried out. It was the first
time I had followed her advice and urging without having my
heart in it.

I was again invited to Rungstedlund, and while my wife was
sick and in hospital, I again stayed for some weeks in April and
May and wrote poetry and worked on my long-planned dissertation on the pioneers of modern lyric poetry, the one I was
supposed to work on in Bonn. A major debate on vivisection
received at this time a great deal of public attention throughout
the country and it occupied our attention considerably. Whether
it concerned animals in captivity or animals as victims of scientific experiments, we had often in our conversations touched on
modern society's ruthless contempt for the peculiar nature and

integrity of animals. Both of us were of the conviction that it was an inadmissible infringement and that we were dealing with a fantastic underestimation of animals' emotions and consciousness and therefore of their suffering during the experiments. I had studied the subject rather thoroughly, and already as a boy I had been introduced to it by my father who was a passionate opponent of vivisection. Karen Blixen regarded it as the equivalent of torture and just as reprehensible, even more so because as human beings we had a responsibility to animals because of our unrestrained superiority to them. She thought it was disgraceful and indefensible for people to safeguard their health at the price of inconceivable, sometimes utterly unnecessary, suffering inflicted on animals. To use an expression fundamental to her concept of life, she considered it to be without honor.

The University of Aarhus had arranged a debate on the subject. Karen Blixen had been invited and had agreed to go. She had written out her contribution, but her health was unstable and she became ill just as she was to leave for Aarhus. I was down with influenza at the same time; the house was like a hospital for poor Mrs. Carlsen, but we both got to our feet to discuss the matter. Karen Blixen proposed that I go to Aarhus and present her contribution on her behalf inasmuch as it was, to a large extent, a result of our conversations and our agreement on the subject, and that I should participate in the discussion both as her representative and in my own capacity. On the other hand, she thought that I was still rather weak and she was a bit apprehensive about my health. The next morning before I got up, I received a check for my travel expenses and a letter in which she said that she could get me a ride to town

in the event that you want to go to Aarhus *yourself*, not just as *my* envoy! Last night I thought of what you have written on the subject and decided that you perhaps

even before you finish your doctoral thesis would like
to stand up against the medical researchers and for
Goethe, Hölderlin, and Pasop! As you know, I cannot
quite forget my responsibility for your health and it
makes me very sad when you do not feel well. But the
last thing in the world that I want to do is clip your
wings—and particularly in connection with this cause.
Do now as the spirit moves you.

I had no doubt that the spirit that moved me was Karen
Blixen's, and so that same morning, April 23, I journeyed to
Aarhus.

I traveled to Aarhus and to Bonn in the same manner, volun-
tarily. I had myself to want to go. Again, she touched the very
core of our relationship: I must spontaneously wish what she
wished and if I had difficulty grasping it, that was just too bad.
It was formally complicated and often intricately expressed, but
the core was very simple. At last, in her concern for my health,
she was worried about clipping my wings and she presumed
that although the wings were mine it was she who controlled
them.

The Lord knows I felt self-conscious when I stood up and
delivered her greeting, but the subject itself soon cured me of
all shyness and gave me assurance when I read my contribution
and then took part in the discussion. Karen Blixen was utterly
delighted when I reported to her on my return. Bonn would
now become the more serious test flight.

IN BONN ❧ ❧ ❧ ❧ ❧ ❧ ❧

I LEFT for Bonn on May 19, 1951, the anniversary of my concussion in Paris almost to the day. Karen Blixen had gone off to Greece on the third of May with Knud W. Jensen* and his wife. My preparations for my departure seemed exactly as meaningless as I had imagined they would be. I was at home at Sletten, enraptured with the poetic work I was doing and had other red-hot irons in the fire. I was happy with my family, and spring was coming in through all the doors and windows of the house. What in the world was I doing going off on this wild-goose chase? But take off I did. The wheels of the train as it passed through northern Germany kept hammering out on the rails my mental condition in rhythms and words for idiocy and foolishness; the wheels thumped out the text from Schubert's *Die Winterreise*, which the Baroness again and again that cold spring, particularly just before we parted, had turned into a chorus describing her own state of mind: *"Welch' ein törichtes Verlangen treibt mich in / die Wüsteneien?"* (What stupid urge then drives me to seek the wilderness?). It suited the undertaking far better than the *"Marseillaise."*

I went off to Bonn with my wife's consent and approval, I have come to realize later, because she preferred to have me there rather than at Rungstedlund—just as Karen Blixen preferred to have me there rather than with my wife at Sletten. About this time my wife had written to a friend about Rungstedlund in these terms: "This house that is completely hostile to me is only ten kilometers from here." Her feeling was not strange, considering that she had heard in a roundabout way that the Baroness

---

*Knud W. Jensen (1916–   ), essayist, wealthy businessman, and amateur of the arts, founder of Louisiana, the fine Danish museum of modern art. —Tr.

would agree to remain in Denmark only if I stayed more or less permanently at Rungstedlund. At the time I had no inkling of this, and whether or not it was true, it undoubtedly had its effect.

At the University of Bonn, overcrowded and still under reconstruction after the devastations of World War II, it was obvious that nobody knew what to do with me. I was quartered in a dormitory for eight, in a sort of waiting room with other foreign students in the same situation, and we smoked, drank, and talked every night into the early morning hours. I spent the days trotting through Kafkaesque corridors and attempting to explain my presence, being referred from one authority to the next, alternating between vague promises of a room and despairing ironic shrugs. "We would prefer to throw out all grantees," one associate professor said outright. After these words I betook myself from Bonn to a tavern in Siebengebirge, stayed there a few days, and walked alone, happy in the vast, fresh mountain forests. It was a veritable convalescence after the dusty and noisy city. I then returned to Bonn, got a room, and tried to sort everything out. It was a difficult moment for the university; nobody had any time for anything and to feel oneself a nuisance was unavoidable. With renewed force the question again presented itself: "Why in the world am I here?" Within a few weeks the possibilities for worthwhile study had been tried out and exhausted. None of the lectures were relevant to my theme, and the libraries were still only halfway usable. I pulled myself together, wrote Karen Blixen a straightforward letter saying exactly how things were, and asked her if I could come to stay at Rungstedlund now instead of after the summer session as planned. The answer, dated June 12, 1951, came quickly:

Dear Magister,

What can I say in answer to your letter but that all doors at Rungstedlund are wide open to you?

And then that I beseech you: do not let me, by this confirmation of our old agreement, become a party to or give my consent to anything that in any human relationship could diminish your sense of honor. Feel free to put the word "honor" in quotation marks. It is old—it is 3,000 years old.

Greetings from everything here.

Yours ever,

KAREN BLIXEN

When I read the letter I regretted very much that I had asked to return. The letter hurt my feelings and confused me, but I should have been prepared for it. In her disappointment, Karen Blixen had to disclaim any and all involvement in my rout, and any responsibility for it, particularly because it was clear from my letter that my heart had never been in the decision to go there in the first place. And she did consider herself involved in that decision. If I could not get my heart into it and find a sensible reason for staying there, she would become involved in the break-off as she had in the decision in the first place—and that she would not do. She appealed, therefore, to my sense of honor so that I would not place her in that position. And that I could, after all, avoid only by staying. Objectively, I understood nothing of all this. To interrupt and leave studies such as these I felt could not detract in the least from my sense of honor, but I had to assure her that it did not. I had expected a yes or a no, not a yes with a condition—a qualified yes. In spite of much indignation and confusion, I was in no doubt what I should answer, and wrote in part:

You must have reasons for requesting me so urgently to consider my sense of honor. You may think that after all I have not considered it, but either I have done nothing but consider it—or I have indeed not considered it. Or else I do not understand anything at all. But after this request to consider my sense of honor, I cannot possibly come to you without degrading it—in one human relationship at least, namely in the one with you.

I immediately felt with all my heart that your request meant that I should not come.

With that letter I considered the case closed and prepared to stay without giving it another thought. A deep tranquillity came over me, perhaps because I finally felt some sort of necessity in it, and I got down to work on an article about Morten Nielsen that I had promised to write a long while before. But a few days later, on June 19, I received a telegram that once again changed everything: PLEASE COME RUNGSTEDLUND. TANIA. I took it to be an expression of understanding and wrote to her how happy I was and that I would reason no more but would come as quickly as possible. The next day yet another letter dated June 18 arrived from Karen Blixen. The letter must have been mailed before the telegram was sent. In it she expounded on what she meant by honor in general and on mine in particular:

> In the latest issue of *Heretica* is an article by Torben
> Monberg,* "Poetry and Magic" (*Poesien og det Magiske*),
> which has occupied my mind a great deal and has set
> me wondering. The author emphasizes the close kinship
> between modern lyrical writing and primitive peoples'
> magic poetry and the extent to which magic metaphors
> make for a distinctive style. Both kinds of poetic works
> unite man and nature. It would be too much to delve
> into it here; I suppose you have a copy yourself and can
> read it. In one passage he compares the Eskimo's making
> himself one with the keen-eyed bird and a poem,

*Torben Monberg (1929–   ), professor of cultural sociology and chief inspector at the Ethnographic Collection of the Danish National Museum. —Tr.

approximately parallel in form, by Paul la Cour.* Both
poems are magic, he says.

What astonishes me is that he can think magic can
be made without faith. *Live* magically—I have always
thought—*be* magical, then you can write magic poetry.
But magic poetry cannot be made according to a cate-
chism or a textbook on aesthetics, which to me is what
Fragments of a Diary (*Fragmenter af en Dagbog*) now seems
to be. To live magically requires faith.

I do know a little about primitive peoples and their
dances and songs; I know with what extreme seriousness and immense tradition they are performed. Magic
and heritage go together—connections with the dead
(who have not become at all malevolent!) and the past. I
also know something about being one with nature. For
the Eskimo it has been a matter of life and death that it
rains and to be able to make a fire and to find water. I
can forget—what Martin A. Hansen and Paul la Cour
probably cannot forget—what day of the week or what
time it is, but not where the cardinal points of the
compass are, or which way the wind blows, or which
phase the moon is in, or whether we need rain or dry
weather.

In connection with this, but also with what we
talked about concerning mystical and moral values, I
have arrived at the view that the moral expression of the
mystical (or the magical), or the mystical in the moral,
is what I call honor. It is an enormous obligation, not
exactly to other persons—although it also must show or
manifest itself in relation to other persons—but to
God, to God's idea of us. At night Peter says to Rosa

* Paul la Cour (1902–1956), lyric poet and art critic. As the author of
Fragments of a Diary (1948), he greatly influenced the views of his generation
on the nature of poetry. —Tr.

that the animal is faithful to God's idea of it, but that
he cannot be faithful himself.

These modern writers—Martin A. Hansen, Paul
la Cour, Ole Wivel—speak so much of the mystical
but they have no faith; they are, in my view, without
honor—or they are utterly without shame. That is also
why in Denmark I am most comfortable in the manor
houses; the nobility's morals are to some extent mystical; they have at least some sense of honor.

In this connection I have thought of something else,
something that pertains to you. Caritas' American friend
said that I was tough—like Christ. Alas, how infinitely
less tough I am than he. I always feel that all I can tell
a person is: "You are worried and upset about many
things, but only one thing is needed." But when the
answer comes, "That's easy for you to say, but eggs
become utterly hardboiled if you leave them on the
fire," I let it get the better of me and I hold my tongue.
Christ did not do that.

And what I really wanted to say to you in my previous letter was exactly this: "You are worried and upset
about many things, but only one thing is needed." It is
utterly unimportant that the concrete mixer makes noise
or that the libraries are closed or that you are treated
like a freshman. One thing you need to decide: Will
your stay in Bonn serve God's idea of you, what one
might call your mission in life? The Stigmatists served
God's idea with Saint Francis. And you have, after all,
sought the aid of people to get to Bonn. If they ask
you, can you honestly tell the same people why you
returned from Bonn? That it was not intended that I
stay in Bonn, it was contrary to my calling?

From your letter today I get the impression that you
can do that. It is not because of all the inconveniences

and troubles you described to Clara or to me in your
first letter that you will terminate your stay in Bonn.
You feel this way about it: 'I went to Bonn blindly,
against the will of God, but I was called home to Rungstedlund.' And if that is so, I can only repeat what I
wrote: 'All our doors are open to you.' Then you are not
running away from something, you are coming to something and therefore you can safely assure me that you come
with honor, and I will think of something that says:
'The victory belongs to the man who draws strength
from defeat.'

This letter has turned out to be poor and confused,
but I have, so help me God, not been able to write a
better one; I have been interrupted by several sets of
callers and by telephone calls. I hope to God you may
derive something from it. One thing I can say is that
I would be very glad if you came. And if you feel as
I think you do, send me a telegram, "Arriving Rungstedlund Sunday evening."

All best wishes—and pardon the poor letter. I mean
well by you. I have made a kind of arbor in the garden;
it is called "The Magister's Closet." If you come we
shall go up there and I shall take more time and explain
it better to you.

As I reread this letter today I can hardly understand my
reaction to it at the time. For all practical purposes it expressed
approximately what I wanted her to understand. But I swung
back to the state of mind I was in after her first letter and wrote
that I could not come because the question of whether I could
come with honor had been posed again and still was an open
question. I could not answer the question and I did not know
what my sense of honor was, at least not in this case. I suppose I
was too exhausted mentally to receive or to give any further

explanation. What I really knew was only that I would not for the *second* time act with the reservations of uncertainty, as I had done by going to Bonn in the first place and that it was better to stay and to make it a one-time affair and not add insult to injury. I sent my regrets in an express letter and it arrived just at the time Karen Blixen expected me, some time in the evening, and, as she wrote in her next letter, with the lights on in various places, so that I should be able to see light on in the house by whatever way I approached it.

During my stay in Bonn, I had made friends with a delightful red-headed, freckle-faced Irishman, a giant, witty, sociable fox, a definite skeptic, a hater of Goethe, art, and music. In spite of the great differences between us or perhaps because of them, we were strongly drawn to each other and were together constantly. His skepticism toward everything was not, as is so often the case, opportunistic and insinuating, but rare in being completely open and consistently Mephistophelian. He taught me to drink beer and, as he lived at the opposite end of town, he often spent the night at my place under a couple of overcoats with his briefcase under his head, snarling a bit in his sleep like a restless poodle. I mentioned our fellowship and characterized him in a letter to Karen Blixen in these words, "an unusual afflicted skeptic with a peculiarly beautiful smile. In him the end has come long ago, so he laughs across the ruins, because he may as well laugh. I can become just as unhappy in one place as in another, he says, when I ask him where he will continue his life after the completion of his studies."

While she sat and waited for me, Karen Blixen got to thinking of how thoughtless it was of her not to ask me to bring my Irishman along to Rungstedlund. She wrote:

> Your poodle, your itinerant scholar, your Mephistopheles could have stayed in the pink room and I would have entertained him so that you could work in peace. Besides, I have been offered a bottle of genuine whis-

key and I assume that all three of us could have had
some pleasant talks in between.

I had been to town all day long, by the way, for a
very funny reason I will tell you about when I write
again—and I was tired, perhaps that was why I got so
annoyed at my negligence that at last I thought: if I
could talk to the Magister now, I would say, "Either
come with your Irish friend, with the demon from
Bonn, or stay away altogether." I calculated that this
really could not be carried out considering that already
you would have been on the train through Germany, on
the ferry across the Great Belt and again on the train
from Korsør and from the central station. Yet I continued to imagine—if you should engage in witchcraft
at all, and, moreover, would have the strength to perform it, you could presumably give the witchcraft retroactive power.

It is characteristic of Karen Blixen that after having specu-
lated about the possibilities of witchcraft, she turns to one of the
most beautiful blessings of the Bible and adds, "I now wish that
in Bonn the Lord bless you and keep you, lift his countenance
upon you and give you peace." She meant both, the witchcraft
as well as the blessing, with equal strength and it is certain that
a theologian ruled in the male half of her soul in carefree and
fantastic sovereignty with all the stops open. It shows again at
the close of the letter: "I place you now as a seal on my hand, as a
seal on my arm and I admonish mighty Bonn's little demons—
with the exception of your Irish friend: 'Who dares to curse
when I will bless?'"

In this letter, unlike the previous one, there was no doubt
that I was now doing the only right thing. Not one word about
my honor. Understanding and consent was unwavering. But
there was a proposal in it that I should go to my German
professors and offer to give lectures because the conditions given

me were really only suitable for a student and were beneath my dignity. I should say, "My best efforts and ability and my time are at your disposal. I can lecture on Danish literature, on Hölderlin or Rilke or on the difficulties of life in general, perhaps also on the means of grace pertaining thereto." And she added: ". . . do not declare immediately that this is pure nonsense, but think it over for a quarter of an hour."

However long I thought about it, such an action was impossible for me partly because I preferred to live my life as an understatement, hidden and at that time still in an attitude of preparation, and partly because I felt such an application would be an intrusion and completely unrealistic. Something of the sort might have been possible in the years before World War I, a time with communications open across all borders, a time Karen Blixen still lived in when style and conventions in general mattered, except when she chose to break through them with sympathetic or diabolic genius. Or it might have been possible after the subsequent student rebellions, but just not at the time in question—as I wrote to her. Conscientiously, I did put out a feeler and found to my relief that it was as impossible as I had imagined. In this matter, therefore, I had to give Karen Blixen a new disappointment after averting the previous one. Much more so because not only could she read between the lines in my answers how absurd I thought the suggestion was, but also because I wrote bluntly that I would not have lectured even if I had been permitted to.

On the whole, my stay in Bonn had attained a dimension my common sense protested against: honor, lectures, God's idea, which had nothing to do with the manner in which I normally understood relationships. More than ever before I was determined to go my own way, to follow my own head without letting my thoughts be distracted by the purpose of the grant (many have done that), Karen Blixen's plans, and God's possible thoughts about my sojourn which I could not make out anyway. To me it was pure convalescence. I began really to feel fine, and I met a young medical student, whose elixir of life was Hölderlin and Rilke and who introduced me to the works of Gottfried Benn, whose suggestive trancelike cynicism I could not stand at first but which later for a while affected me strongly. My friend suffered from a split between his profession and poetry, a split which was healed occasionally only by his laughing enthusiasm. I now divided my time between him, the Irishman, and a group studying Kierkegaard and wandering about the mountains or along the banks of the Rhine. I discovered that I had placed far too much importance on whether I happened to be here or there. Yes, spontaneously I arrived at the formulation from the Baroness' "Ritual for a Choice": that in practice it was of exceptionally little importance. In this relaxed mood, with no noteworthy deeds to report on, I slipped out of Karen Blixen's imagination and her thoughts concerning me. I suspect that my life, no more honorable than ignominious, bored her; but also that that was not the reason I should stay away from Rungstedlund. Later, when I read through the letters of this period, I found a precious comment on the letters and the entire situation, the grand total of her comprehension, after the blessings and after she in all probability had become just as tired as I was of the problems of honor. On the top of my first letter of regret she had written:

> The meaning of this letter really is (See the following letters):
> "I did not feel I was having a good time in Bonn; so I would rather be at Rungstedlund where I thought I would enjoy it more. But it now seems to me that I will not enjoy it as much at Rungstedlund as I thought I would and in the meantime I am getting along much better in Bonn than I previously was. Therefore, I now prefer to stay here."

That was not exactly what I had expected. And yet it is illuminating at any rate. We were out of touch with each other and for a while almost ceased to exchange letters. But there was another reason for losing touch.

The proposal in Karen Blixen's reply to my letter of regret was followed by another important passage:

> Your letter made me glad for yet another reason. It gave
> me the impression that you are in love. If so, you must
> tell me, for you owe me that also, as I shall explain to
> you if we meet again. Whatever the others may think,
> I have always thought that you had the capacity for it.

If we had kept in real touch with each other, she would never have been mistaken on this point. So I had to give her yet another disappointment, the third one I had caused her from Bonn, and I really felt quite embarrassed to say that neither in honor nor in adventure was I able to live up to her expectations: I had not fallen in love. Her certainty that I was in love was therefore not due to that parapsychical insight I had experienced time and again, but to her *wish* that it should happen to me, just as the whole Bonn expedition had come about more by her impassioned wish than by unbiased insight. Besides that, I think it was the only deeper and unexpressed reason she could accept for my last change of mind and refusal to go to Rungsted-lund. Otherwise it must have seemed incomprehensible to her after I had so forcefully provoked the invitation, was expected, and my honor had been reinterpreted to mean: come back. How certain she was is seen from the postscript to the letter: "Can the attractions in Bonn keep you from going to London some time within the next six weeks to see *Antony and Cleopatra?*"

I was not in love then, but near the end of my stay I did fall in love with a Danish friend of mine and of the Baroness who was already married and under such circumstances that I did not feel it reasonable to tell about it for a while or to mention it in a letter. This was the second reason for the long break in our correspondence.

My wife had coolly pulled away from me when I sought her support during my mental skid because she felt she had troubles enough of her own. Karen Blixen had wanted me to be in some faraway place where adventure waited, some tremendous ecstasy, in short: the fire was built, lightning struck from the blue sky, and when I saw this old friend our friendship changed into love. It developed on long enraptured walks in the countryside around Goslar, in Siebengebirge, and along the Rhine and lovely evenings of dancing. We deceived ourselves right up to the day of her departure about what it all meant. Then it dawned on us. Nevertheless, we decided to remain faithful to our spouses. And on the platform and in the deserted night afterward, the words of Sophus Claussen rang through me in defiance and blind gratitude: "Let the waters of the flood carry me away—I have lived for one day in Ecbatana." And after that there was only emptiness.

It was an impossible, mad love and it made the whole journey exactly as calamitous and crazy as I felt it to be at the beginning, a real context for the litany by Schubert hammered out by the train wheels on my way to Bonn. I came home changed, secretly stabilized in despair and bliss without end, indifferent to everything else. Karen Blixen was both more remote and closer than she used to be because she knew nothing of what had happened to me and yet I—we—felt that she was precisely the mighty genie and latent protectress of our love. This I simply assumed, but this time it was I who was mistaken.

Clara, who with all her heart had wanted me to go to Bonn, followed the experiment with attentive concern, as her letter of June 11, 1951, indicates:

Dear Thorkild,

Today the Baroness came home with a big harvest of clover—about twenty-four with more than three leaves—from four-leaf up to seven-leaf. There were two seven-

leaf clovers, and she asked me to send them to you.
They are enclosed.

The Baroness thinks a great deal about you; I do not
know why she has not written. (The other night I think
you literally appeared before her! How it actually took
place I cannot quite explain because I have no experience with that kind of event.) Perhaps one of the reasons that she has been unable to write is that we have
had a bad accident here. Nils [Mrs. Carlsen's small son]
and little Helge [the gardener's son] were hit by a car
and are in hospital. . . . It was a terrible moment when
they both lay here unconscious—and Mrs. Carlsen—
well, I shall spare you further shocking details and
merely say that it looks as if the two little fellows will
escape permanent injury. . . .

I must pull myself together to ask a few friends in
Bonn if they have any connections that might be useful
to you. Now that you *are* there.

Incidentally, I am sorry to have been a party to
chasing you off now that I hear that it is so unpleasant
down there and I see that the Baroness misses you so
much.

Last night it caught my eye that my blessed candle
from Candlemas, like the one you have, is placed directly below the Spanish Madonna that resembles the
Baroness. . . . I have introduced a little ceremony:
every evening the candle will be lit for a moment and
then will be offered the Lord's Prayer and Hail Mary
and the little prayer from the litany of Loreto, "*Mater
Boni Consilii, ora pro nobis*" (Mother of Good Counsel,
pray for us) to lend you a helping hand. This kind of
papistic stuff is the best *I* can come up with. I think
everything will work out all right for you in Bonn, also
with respect to storks. "With respect to storks" is an
allusion to the story in *Out of Africa* about the man who

was guided along strange roads and fell into abominable
ditches and finally, by evening, saw that his route
formed the picture of a beautiful stork. I am sure you
remember it.

I do not know if my journey formed exactly the picture of a
stork, let alone a beautiful one, but I suppose the picture of
some sort of bird emerged from it, although oddly frayed at the
edges. Clara was not the only one who interceded for me. One
of the most important characters at Rungstedlund did also,
namely Pasop. In her next letter Clara wrote:

On the other hand, faithful Pasop works hard on his
little prayer rug to help you stick it out. Under these
trying circumstances the priest has taken an understanding attitude to his crashing all the way into the
sanctuary, even in the middle of mass.
    Greetings from the Garden of Eden and from your
involuntary tormentor,

CLARA

Various rather impressive ceremonies were thus being performed at home for the benefit of my soul. Unlike the Baroness,
I did, however, consider Clara absolutely blameless in the matter and its incomprehensible dimensions. On the subject of
four-leaf clovers, Karen Blixen possessed a fabulous ability to
spot them, even without bending over while walking or kneel-
ing down from an upright position. I never succeeded in finding
a four-leaf clover whether I was lying with my nose in the grass
or trying with a bird's-eye view. It is true that she insisted she
had poor eyesight and that might be correct in other respects,
but I think she had some kind of magic or mental bead in front
of her eye which trained it accurately on the very first knife-
edge-thin, almost invisible new moon, or on each four-leaf
clover.

MORE ABOUT THE PACT ✄ ✄ ✄

AFTER my return from Bonn I again spent an autumn at Rungstedlund, but I was not as unconcernedly acquiescent as I had been the previous fall and my stay was shorter. This time a long-term isolation from my family and friends could not be for reasons of convalescence; it had to be based solely on the necessity of a quieter working environment than I could find at home. This was a flimsy excuse because I had excellent working conditions there also, although the magic atmosphere of Rungstedlund was, of course, missing. With my great new love I preferred to be anywhere but at home, and Karen Blixen simply wanted me to live at Rungstedlund; she thought it was best for me and best for both of us. On one occasion she gave me the old gramophone Denys Finch-Hatton had given her because, she said, since those days she had not listened to so much music with anybody as with me. On another occasion, she gave me her painting of the young Kikuyu girl. I did not take these gifts too seriously; I regarded them as a kind of Spanish grandiosity toward her guest. But it turned out that there was another side to it. One day when she mentioned the painting again, she asked me solemnly if I could consider taking over Rungstedlund and living there always, inasmuch as none of her relatives wanted it after her death. "If you could do that, I would bequeath you Rungstedlund." Rather shaken, I tried to take her offer as a joke, but with no success. Honestly frightened, I turned it down. I could see that it was a moving and generous way of permanently consolidating our relationship, but I was neither enough of an adventurer nor practical enough to accept.

At the same time Karen Blixen intensified her interference in my life, perhaps under the impression that I was not as spontaneously and undividedly present as I had been in the past. She began to refer to the pact on various occasions, specifically to the form of it she had sketched in her long letter to me in Paris. But to no good use, and what was I to do with my shortcomings in that connection? I was not humble and simple like Rosa and I did not possess the unequivocal allegiance of Pasop or the stability and grandezza of Farah. Despite periods of ecstatic and inspired assurance, I was of an impassioned and awkward, irresolute nature, full of contradictions, easily moved to hubris and to gloom. I aspired after wisdom and rose to my best in humor and affection. All in all, I matured late and my mind was filled with immense amounts of unclassified material that might be regarded as potentialities, which undoubtedly attracted my prophetess, whom I thought I needed far more than I could ever imagine she might need me. This, too, she knew precisely and she demanded in return, almost with an Old Testament zeal, that I should have no other gods before her. In her dark hours of intolerance, she considered it a misunderstanding and a forsaking that I had strong human associations also outside Rungsted-lund, and though she might never admit it openly, she did let me know this indirectly and emphatically. It was not that I should have no connections whatever with other people, but they should be conventional and reverent and, moreover, of an adventurous and noncommittal kind. I should maintain an integrity based solely and fundamentally on my relationship with her, that is, on our pact. In the beginning she had tactfully shown much respect for my marriage and she had felt that it was endangered by my coarseness and lack of consideration for my wife. She said that with respect to my more delicate and far more refined wife, I behaved like one "who drove nails with a violin." As time went on she regarded this marriage as a nuisance and a misunderstanding, a drag and a hindrance to what she considered my destiny. After she had wanted to turn the journey to Paris into a kind of honeymoon for us, she ignored it deliberately and unmercifully. When I was not at Rungstedlund, she wanted me any place other than at home, preferably somewhere on my travels. As I have said, she also had plans that we should go together to England, to Stratford-on-Avon to see *Antony and Cleopatra*. She loved that particular play and had tickets for it from John Gielgud, whom she wanted me to meet. Another time we were to go to Stockholm to see a performance of the *Oresteia* and on a third occasion to Venice. But the anchor-point was and remained Rungstedlund, and from there she wrote to me while I was in Bonn:

> When my roses are in bloom or the new moon is in the sky behind the chestnut trees, I feel it unnatural that you are not here to share them and I have wished— indeed believed—that you could have managed it without any kind of split mind.

I did have a cleft mind. I had told Karen Blixen and written to her that I felt partly that she made too much of it and partly that she too often presumed that no split existed at all. It was a fact, but it could be overcome temporarily when I wrote and was in love, through friendship and work and contact with nature. Clearly, Karen Blixen counted on the pact as a means to conquer this cleavage and she plainly felt the lack of a conclusive victory over it as a failure. She would come up with the most peculiar things for reinforcement and confirmation of the pact. She gave me, for example, an Indian coat her father had got in trade from the Indians in the forests of Wisconsin: "It will be good for you to wear when you sit and work, warm in the winter and cool in the summer, but this you will know, that if you are ever unfaithful to me while wearing it, it will burn you like a Nessus shirt." And another thing she gave me: Above the door in the green room she hung a piece of wood with an inscribed text that she had quoted often to me—as the second formula for our pact—which under all circumstances and vicissitudes should remain in force. Sometimes she exchanged "I" for "you" as in the past; at others, she said that when I looked at it and read it I should think, with trust beyond measure, that this was how it was between her and me:

> If I take the wings of the morning
> and dwell in the uttermost parts of the sea,
> even there shall thy hand lead me,
> and thy right hand shall hold me.

Karen Blixen calmly put herself in God's place when she felt it necessary. As in the quotation from Heiberg's play, she did so when she was without her faith in God and was unable to believe, for example, in me, but on the contrary thought that I, in my insufficiency and in periods of exceptional exposure, needed protection and somebody to believe in: in her. Or when she was seized by the overwhelming jealousy characteristic of Jehovah and the Greek gods: an annihilating jealousy without shame or restraint, but with the marks of innocence and the right to exercise it. If she hid it and controlled it in any way, she would do so for strategic reasons alone, not because she was in doubt about her right to feel it. In apparent masked objectivity it would show itself for example as definite disapproval. I wrote a letter I did not see again until I was setting down these recollections in which, along with Christmas greetings, I told her how I was going to celebrate Christmas at home with friends and music and under the sign of the Christ child. Across the top of this letter in her large beautiful hand is written: IDIOT. This was the opposite of the stern and awe-inspiring generosity with which she said and sang, "Who dares to curse, when *I* will bless?"

She edited the text not just in this case where she changed the "You" that applied to God to "I" or "I" to "You" as in the passage of scripture; it happened in a like manner on another occasion. To explain to her that it did not necessarily mean a split mentality or a breach in the pact that I spent time with my family, with my wife and son, who most certainly meant much to me, as well as with my friends, relatives, and other connections, but that I could still keep a course toward God and fulfill a possible destiny, no matter what kind of destiny it might be, I presented her with one of Franz Werfel's aphorisms from his *Theologumena*. It was an autumn evening during my second stay; we sat talking by the fireside. Already at that time I felt the aphorism, which I had carefully translated with this presentation in mind, to be a bit formidable for the occasion, but I could use it to explain not simply my present situation but what I hoped would some day become my permanent situation:

> God speaks only to the oldest souls, to those that have lived and suffered longest: You shall belong to no one and to nothing, to no party, no majority, no minority, no community even if it serves me at my altar. You shall not belong to your parents nor to your wife nor your children nor to your brothers and sisters, nor to those who speak your language no more than to those who speak another language and least of all to yourself. You shall belong only to *me* in this world. But how could you be mine, except by living unobtrusively in your world like everybody else and yet not belonging to it?

The reason that this aphorism impressed me so strongly at the time, in spite of its theological form, was that fundamentally it had something to do with wisdom. A wisdom that came from Christianity of course, but one that was post-Christian so to speak, a possible Western wisdom.

After I had read it to her, she asked to read it herself. I handed her the paper, on which she concentrated a long time. Then she nodded, took a pencil, wrote something on the paper at the top and at the bottom, and handed it back to me. I was greatly astonished by what I saw. She had crossed out the word *God* and had written *I* above it—and below the aphorism she had signed her name and thus had turned it into yet another formula for our pact. If the aphorism was formidable enough in itself, her rewriting it was hubris of no lesser degree and the entire situation the expression of an extreme *folie à deux*.

THE WORLD OUTSIDE 🐟🐟🐟🐟

A CHANGE of another sort had also taken place. Karen Blixen had previously wanted me to be as inconspicuous at Rungstedlund as I was when I traveled. Now she wanted me to face the public on my own, and especially in her company, since she had often imagined that some day we should appear together in the history of literature. Hence her suggestion that I give lectures in Bonn. In this second autumn at Rungstedlund, this wish of hers also found other expression, one of which was rather grotesque and came as a complete surprise.

One afternoon as I sat in the green room and worked on my poem "The Raven" (*Ravnen*), there was suddenly a knock on the door and Karen Blixen stepped in with a group of teachers from the Teachers' College. She wanted to show them the "Poet's Room," as she called it, and introduce them to the poet who sat there working as Johannes Ewald once sat and worked in a room at the other end of the house. Perhaps some day it might also be remembered and mentioned in the history of literature that I had worked in this room. I looked up from my papers and felt as if the chair suddenly had been pulled out from under me—and as if the wall, behind which I thought I was unseen and protected, suddenly turned out to be a stage curtain that had gone up. And now someone, the last person I would have expected, stood there and recited the prologue to the play. Gone was the innocence that belongs as much to a happy workroom as it does to a boy's den or to the starry sky.

In my self-consciousness and embarrassment, I did not know where to look. My secret closet had suddenly become a platter, but thank heaven just then a tray with sherry and glasses was brought in and saved the situation. After the toast to welcome my blameless spectators, who luckily were more interested in the cosmopolitan producer, we all walked to Ewald's Hill where Karen Blixen gave a little speech. When I got back to the green room, I found my papers scattered as by a sudden gust of wind. I felt deprived of the invisibility that had been such a happy precondition for work and that had been strongly emphasized by Karen Blixen herself during my past visits. Had she herself not written, "I think you have been looked at too much"? Shortly after this incident she fell ill, and from the other end of the house she sent me "Converse at Night in Copenhagen." The tale and the note that accompanied it made me very happy and I thought that now there was an opportunity to express how greatly I enjoyed the tale and how deeply it had moved me and at the same time to say what I thought of the recent unexpected visit. It had left me unusually dejected and doubtful, and I wanted to get it out of my system, to clear up everything between us. My answering note was just as exaggerated and unreasonable as my dejection, but in essence correct, I think to this day.

I wrote in part: "I would like to cooperate with the Baroness in everything, and I will be more than happy to receive visitors in my room, being proud of such trust, but not in my 'Poet's Room.'" And I went on to the effect that my peace and security had been disturbed and, with reference to the letter she wrote me in Paris, that I felt "intensely hampered by being looked at too much," that I felt caught precisely by what I wanted to escape and, furthermore, that I was ashamed that I could not rise above it all. "Rather than prematurely wrap about me a myth which under the eyes of others did not feel like a coronation robe but more like a straight jacket," I wrote, "the Baroness may for a whole week tie Pasop on a bear chain outside my bedroom door.—I am glad, however, that you call me 'Magister.'" (Implied: and not a poet.) The remark about Pasop refers to my hypochondriacal sleeping habits and his restlessness in the mating season. But Karen Blixen was not in the mood for a joke and when she appeared again a few days later, I got as good as I gave. There was not one iota of understanding, not one hint of her possibly having been at fault; on the contrary, she considered me silly and unreasonable and said that I should think of the far worse things of this nature that she had had to endure. She said, in conclusion, "You really must learn to grin at the Devil as I have done; God only knows how many times the Devil grins at you." Our disagreement resembled the one about my giving lectures in Bonn: I could not deal with "the world" in that manner. I had aptitude neither for asserting myself in public nor for saying no. Karen Blixen was better at the former than the latter, and the way that she handled it certainly impressed me, but the merry cynicism in her manner I could not match, neither then nor since. Clara came in just at this point to report that there was a call requesting the Baroness to speak or read her stories on a certain occasion. "Thank them and tell them I will be glad to do it," said the Baroness and then shouting at Clara, who was already halfway through the door, "But remember to call and cancel it the day before!"

It was difficult for Karen Blixen to forgive me that I had tainted my letter of reply to "Converse at Night" by my petty disapproval and foolish if not presumptuous reproach because of the visit to the green room. She felt that I had returned unreasonableness and hard feelings for generosity and trust, and in a way that was true. Some time later it occurred to me that perhaps she sent me the tale just then because she had sensed my dejection over the incident, which in my mind should have been relegated to the category of high comedy. But it was also a symptom. More and more often in our relationship, heavenly sweetness crossed with human bitterness.

But Karen Blixen also wanted me to face the world outside Rungstedlund. One afternoon she explained to me in detail how restrictive and inhibiting my environment was, both the provincial one I came from and the literary one I was now in. She revealed a plan she had that she and I together should visit and talk with some of the most important men and women of the time, Agnes Henningsen and Vilhelm Andersen, Hartvig Frisch* and Niels Bohr, John Gielgud, Aldous Huxley, and Albert Schweitzer. In short, she was to bring about my introduction to the world. All that came of this notion was a visit to Vilhelm Andersen. He was big, warm, and friendly, but to me the situation was absurd and I was determined that it should not be repeated. I would assert myself with my own work and with my own person, on my own terms. I would gladly meet important people in natural ways, but not as a protégé. The next visit was to be with Niels Bohr. But I thought of Blake, who says, "No bird soars too high if it soars with its own wings." But the bird that flies not with its own wings does.

---

*Agnes Henningsen (1868–1962), author and early champion of women's rights; Vilhelm Andersen (1864–1953), literary historian, professor at the University of Copenhagen 1908–1930; Hartvig Frisch (1893–1950), philologist, cultural historian, and politician, Social Democratic member of Parliament 1926–1950, minister of education 1947–1950. —Tr.

THE JEALOUS MATCHMAKER 🐦 🐦

W HILE my meeting with the world outside was being planned, I met my beloved whenever possible for walks in the Folehave woods. Our love was at its zenith, vibrant and untouchable and yet unconsummated because, in our boundless idealism, we would not insult our spouses. But we had expectations of some miracle that would justify our love somewhat like that which religious believers must expect. It also happened that we met at Rungstedlund at a dinner party arranged by Karen Blixen. To this party she had invited Frank Jaeger,* whose poems she liked very much, and Jørgen Gustava Brandt, who, greatly fascinated by the Baroness, had begun to come to Rungstedlund while I was in Bonn. There was also my friend, whom Karen Blixen thought very lovely and whom she regarded as one of her "daughters." That evening I was bubbling over with happiness. Karen Blixen was even-tempered and cheerful; her face was smooth and full and had a special radiance. She wore a tight headband and a modern dress that was suited to her age—she did not always do that—and very few jewels. Her beauty had an air of resoluteness and an autumnlike maturity about it. She obviously very much enjoyed being the hostess, and she played the role to the hilt. When she was like this, my affection for her was always at its peak. And my friend sat on my right at dinner. After dinner we sat in a semicircle before the fireplace, which as usual I tended with wood, and on Karen Blixen's suggestion we began to play *bouts rimés*. She and Frank Jaeger were by far the most skillful at it; I was so absent-minded with happiness because of my love's presence that I could hardly concentrate on the game. Later when I took her

*Frank Jaeger (1926–1977), novelist, short-story writer, and lyric poet, translator of Molière, Corneille, and Goethe. —Tr.

home in Karen Blixen's old sports car and parted from her in the brilliant light of a full moon, I thought against all reasonableness and common sense, as in the old fairy tales, that my ship had come in.

The sun and the moon, however, could not stand still, and an earthly decision had to be made. At last the pressure became too great and while I was on a visit to my home at Sletten, my friend confided in Karen Blixen, partly encouraged and confident that the latter had already guessed our love. It is likely that she had suspected something and tentatively had fanned some imagined embers, but she had apparently no idea how advanced the condition was. Perhaps she had counted on my telling her if I fell in love in accordance with the promise she had exacted in one of her letters, but my friend had not wanted me to. Under the impression that Karen Blixen knew anyway, she now told it all (for the same reason and because I thought the time to tell had come, I also told her shortly thereafter, not knowing that my friend had already confided in her). The reaction had been surprisingly vehement, quite contrary to the primeval motherly acquiescence that had been expected, and it shocked my friend and deprived her of all hope. The reaction was more subdued and sorrowful toward me. It took me some time to understand the reasons for it.

Karen Blixen wanted me to fall in love just as the Councilor wants Anders Kube to find love in her tale "The Poet." Although I was very fond of my wife, she did not think my marriage was adequate for my really falling in love. This feeling did not emerge until after my journey to Paris and after she had begun not just to ignore the marriage, but to act as if it did not exist at all. But great love does not make its appearance according to wish and arrangement, invitation, or order. On the contrary, it will nearly always, and particularly when one is well along in life, come uninvited, awkwardly, and at cross purposes to everything; its spontaneity is rebellious and radical. Karen Blixen made no bones about her wish and played with various possibilities. When, for instance, Countess Caritas Bernstorff-Gyldensteen, whom I had seen a few times since we first met and about whom I had been asked my opinion, was to visit Rungstedlund, she would say, "But where will she sleep? How about the bed next to yours? Wouldn't it be lovely to wake up with Caritas' blonde head on the pillow beside you?" I liked the Countess very much, but not in that way.

Karen Blixen sometimes entertained fantasies about herself as the Erlking in Goethe's *Der Erlkönig*, and bitingly and bitterly mocked the idea that he was so evil when he offered the boy his daughters for company. *"Und wiegen und tanzen und singen dich ein,"* (They will rock you and dance you and sing you to sleep), she hummed somberly and seductively and concluded, "And instead the boy wails and thinks he will die!" She also regarded her brother Thomas Dinesen's daughters as her own. *"Meine Töchter* (my daughters)," she called them. She once arranged a luncheon for the two Dinesen girls, Caritas, Clara, herself and me. I was to drive Karen Blixen's old sports coupé to pick up Caritas in Frederiksdal, where she lived with her mother in a small rococo mansion. Just as I was ready to start, Karen Blixen came up to the car with a bouquet of freesias and asked me to step out for a moment. Slowly and meticulously she proceeded to stick the freesias in my hair, which at that time was thick, black, and curly. She walked around me and worked long and patiently on the arrangement, then cheerfully evaluated the result and said joyfully and threateningly, "Don't you dare touch them. I expect them to be right where they are now when you come back with Caritas." I cast a quick glance in the rearview mirror when I started and saw with a mixture of horror and extreme embarrassment my head adorned with freesias. I left, but could not find my way. No less than three times I had to stop, stick my daffy flower-embellished head out the window and ask for directions. The first time I pretended to know noth-

ing of the unusual decoration, the second time I pretended this
was my everyday appearance and nothing to wonder about,
when the person I asked kept looking with fascination above my
eyes. The third time I was becoming immune and stood on my
right to wear freesias in my hair if it pleased me. The flower
children of more recent years may wonder about my embarrassment, but it was not so easy to carry flowers about in this way,
dressed in a normal suit and driving an antiquated sports coupé,
on a Sunday morning on quiet suburban streets at the beginning
of the fifties. I finally got there and Caritas and her mother were
the first people I had met since I had been decorated who did not
so much as hint that there was anything peculiar about my
appearance. They gave me a tour of the mansion and the park
and offered me a glass of sherry before I took off with Caritas. I
told her after a while how much I admired her and her mother
for ignoring the freesias as a matter of course. Caritas laughed
and said she realized immediately that it was "one of Tanne's
gags." Karen Blixen looked at me approvingly when we arrived
at Rungstedlund; then, to my relief, she began to stick freesias
in the hair of Caritas and the daughters who had arrived in the
meantime. It turned out to be a delightful and hilarious luncheon—after one of the most trying mornings I had experienced in a long time.

As I appeared rather coldly disposed toward these and other
suggestions, all of which were introduced and staged with frank
frivolity—she meant them and yet she did not mean them—
and because in these matters I was unimpressionable or good for
nothing but to drive nails with a violin, she began to assert that
I ought to take a snake charmer as a mistress. In any case it
should be a big, strong girl, a type for which Karen Blixen had a
special weakness, and one my clumsiness and lack of polish
could not faze. A type like that would be what I needed to fulfill
my basic (to me undefined) needs, once I had overcome my
passion for the frail and delicate. It was not until I left for Bonn

that these fantasies became alive and, so to speak, geographically placed, if not topographically so. Ominously enough, there was on the outskirts of Bonn a ridge called the Venusberg which in reality is a monotonous, shrubby, swampy area devoid of snake charmers and the like. My Irish friend pointed out that the area's original name was *Vennberg*, that *Venn* meant *swamp* and that by a popular etymological error it had become Venusberg. Without doubt it was Venusberg that my subconscious wayward fantasies had skirted, but what I found in reality was the swamp, yet another sign of the failure of my Bonn expedition. And when I did fall in love in Bonn, it occurred far from Venusberg. I fell in love with a woman of the quality of a Stradivarius, hardly a snake charmer.

Our love could not, of course, remain hidden, and Karen Blixen, to my shocked amazement and my friend's horror, did not regard it as a blessing but as a calamity. It was disastrous in her eyes because my friend was the wrong partner for me and because our respective marriages were threatened. The latter reason especially caught me by surprise. After all the metamorphoses from Athena to the Devil's friend, from Hecate, love's protectress consecrated to the moon, to powerful, daring, and jocular matchmaker and our love's presumed patroness, she now stood as a ratifier of marriage, an angry and sorrowful Hera. Why? When what she, hardly pretending, had hoped for and conjured up had occurred: I was seriously in love. It was obvious that it did not suit her, that it was not what she had in mind and that it was again a disappointment. But why this vehement reaction that even made use of a Hera-like attitude, that seemed to want to negate what had happened, to undo it—to attempt to perform witchcraft with retroactive powers, as she had written with respect to my bringing my Irish friend along to Rungstedlund.

It had struck me in the past that every one of her projects or arrangements that I showed a trace of inclination to engage in earnestly myself had been tabled or terminated, but I had paid little heed to the fact at the time. Now I remembered and understood. Often Karen Blixen did not at all have the nerve or the strength of mind to be confronted with what she herself had implemented. This was one of the reasons things could go wrong, even if they were "objectively" successful. She had reckoned without her monstrous demon of jealousy. I am convinced that this demon could surprise her as much as whomever else she turned it on. I had permission to fall in love; it was good if I did, but, after all, not seriously. It was not just ordinary feminine jealousy that asserted itself; it was the annihilating radical zeal of the Old Testament. I should have no other gods before her. And according to our pact I was hers and nobody else's. If what she, in one aspect as the daring, designing matchmaker, might really wish for her favorite actually came to pass, she had to bring to bear an almighty jealousy against it in another aspect and try to annihilate it. It was a jealousy without conscience and hesitation because it was of a divine nature, above all morals, and, if it was up to her, instantly fatal like the wrath of the gods.

Only then did I understand how insane, how blind it had been to seek where it was last to be found not only the mightiest support hoped for but also the secret confirmation of our rights. It was especially the latter that she wanted to make clear to us. The Hera impulse was to that extent genuine and useful, but it was only a fringe phenomenon, a rationalization after the fact of the flashing, total rejection. It was the first time the childish and unbelievable happiness of those days was laid low. Suddenly I realized how hopeless our case was when measured on the earthly and social scale that we had resolutely rejected because it did not belong to our heaven. In our incessantly repeated, blissful, present moments we had felt the future as something superfluous, a shameful distraction. Now it became the one and only requirement, but a black gaping hole opened where it should have been. Although it sounds contradictory, one might say that we had counted on the future in a straightforward or miraculous way, *if* that future should turn out to become necessary. My internal security collapsed and I was seized by a frantic sorrow that simultaneously broke down my powers of resistance and ability to act and, if possible, amplified my love, now no longer happy and absurdly innocent as before. Karen Blixen must have sensed this, because a few days later she suddenly reversed herself and agreed that what had happened to me was nevertheless something right and wonderful, however bad it might be otherwise. "Can you feel," she said, full of unexpected consideration and confidence, "can you feel it like claws in your heart, as if you are being shaken and tossed about by a wild beast? Oh, I remember it, I recognize it. It is the worst pain of all that exists. No, no, I do not feel sorry for you. I envy you. No, with all my heart I want you to have it." This duality of intense compassion and stern rejection characterized her attitude during the time that followed and made her conduct more inscrutable and labyrinthine than ever. She moved in a completely *unchronological* fashion from one extreme to the other and usually when least expected.

I interrupted my stay at Rungstedlund shortly afterward to tour Norway in the company of several other poets. Clara and the Baroness went with me to the bus stop at Strandvejen, because I had to go to Sletten first to prepare for my departure. Karen Blixen was wearing a hood, and while I waved and saw their forms fade away in the November mist, it seemed to me for one wild, grimly humorous moment that they looked like the old parson and his wife from *The Angelic Avengers*. Since my first happy autumn sojourn, everything had changed. Each paradise clearly has its limits.

THE RUPTURE 🙟🙟🙟🙟🙟

W HEN I returned from Norway, Karen Blixen called me at Sletten, where I was to stay for about a week before going on to Rungstedlund, and requested that we meet at once. She came and picked me up in her car and we drove to Store Kro in Fredensborg for tea. She quickly asked a few questions about the trip to Norway, then suddenly grabbed her bag from the chair beside her, placed it on the table, and pulled out a crumpled letter that she handed me to read. It was a letter to my wife from a friend of hers who ridiculed my extended stays at Rungstedlund and advised her to insist that I move home and that she create equally good working conditions for me there. During a visit to this friend's house, I had seen on the dining-room wall a picture like the one entitled *"Avant l'attaque"* (Before the Attack) that hung above my bed at Rungstedlund. I had commented on it and said jokingly that under that picture I could work anywhere. She hinted at this in the letter and offered to lend it to my wife so that it might hang above my bed at home, if that would improve my working conditions and aid my inspiration. When I was home, before going off to Norway, my wife had mentioned her friend's offer and had given me the letter to take along to read. I read it and then put it away with other letters in a closet or drawer in the green room.

Karen Blixen complained that her friends never would have treated her like this; after this letter she realized that they were people different from me; *they* were people with a code of honor. I answered meekly that I had not written the letter, that the letter had not been written for my eyes, and that I did not agree with its contents even if I had enjoyed reading it. She felt that I did agree because I had placed it among my letters. I said that I was far from agreeing with the contents of every letter I got, not to mention those intended for someone else. When she impatiently cut me off and declared that that was irrelevant, I answered that in the end it had to be a private matter and that I had not dreamt that she, in my absence, would read the letters I had kept. She answered that she had given me a key to the drawer and the closet where I could keep them and when I did not use it to lock them up, I had to accept the fact that she would read them. I disagreed with her and suggested that the difference between her honorable friends and me might be, in part, that she did not read their letters without their knowledge. She said that was unnecessary because they did not receive such letters and that moreover it was irrelevant but that she would like an explanation of this letter's contents. I maintained that apparently my wife's friend felt sorry for my wife because I was home so rarely and that she had chosen to express her feelings in a humorous fashion. Karen Blixen did not find this the least bit funny and continued her interrogation; gradually I felt like a suspect charged with something about which he could say no more than had already been said. In the end, she bitterly asserted that she and her friends might make bad mistakes, but never one of this kind, for they had a code of honor and first and last they always observed inviolably at least the rules of classical tragedy.

It became utterly impossible for me to see any reasonable relation between the crumpled and thoroughly studied letter on the tablecloth between us and her momentous conclusion. I did not think it particularly honorable to go into someone else's drawer and read his mail. I would never have been able to do it myself, but I kept silent about such petty details; this was perhaps a code for which I was ill equipped. Or the Devil's friend had rights not given to everyone. In short, I did not know whether she spoke from a plane dizzyingly high above mine, or from one a good deal below, and I was nauseated with shame and discomfort, but I tried to keep all my feelings at arm's length by

not saying too much—lying prone, so to speak, during the
barrage. She concluded by saying, "The rules of classical tragedy are perhaps the only rules I and my equals, my friends,
really have respected and observed; we know nothing of the pity
and the mess in the Riding Master's world, the one you are
entangled in and from which you apparently cannot free yourself. One of my kind would know that after this we could not see
each other again." This vitriolic whiplash of disdain for my love
for her, as well as the consequence she drew from it all, almost
knocked the wind out of me. After this salvo she rose, but as I
moved to pick up the *corpus delicti*, the unfortunate letter, she
snatched it up in a flash, stuffed it into her bag, and with a
profoundly wronged look declared that she would keep it.

On the way home in her car, I thought the worst was over,
but she began talking about our pact and asked me to cancel it
because she could not do it herself after what had taken place
during my stay in Brittany. "Because *I* cannot do it, *you must.*"
In the meantime, she had pulled over onto the shoulder of the
road at a lonely spot and stopped the car. Her anger had disappeared, her face was smooth, and I saw only her long profile, as
in a somber and sad voice she quoted a stanza I was unfamiliar
with at the time, one that she had written when quite young:

> In its prison my heart sings
> only of wings, only of wings,
> none of the world's other lovely songs
> beautifully ring in its ear.
> Even birds born in cages have dreams
> about freely flying skyward,
> and in its prison my heart sings
> only of wings, only of wings.

She turned abruptly straight toward me, and bleary-eyed,
implored me, as if I had complete power over her fortune or
misfortune: "Release me, release me!" and she kept repeating

these words as if they were the sequence of great dirge, while I was at my wits' end, knowing that if I said "Yes" I would not mean it, and knowing that I could not say "No" either. I found the reason that I should cancel the pact idiotic and incomprehensible. The great love that I had discovered in Bonn had come to a dead end; it began every morning with a hope I could not kill and ended every night with a feeling of loss and void nothing could fill. And now I was to knock down that which, despite all vicissitudes, was just as dear to me, that which I had thought unshakable and untouchable whatever happened, the firm anchor in the confusion and the last place where my self-esteem had a hold: the pact. And I had to reach the decision myself. "Release me," she said again, but I could not answer. I could only ask time to consider—and she turned the key, started the engine, and drove to the edge of Lave Woods, where I got out and said good-bye.

When I got home I felt humbled and crushed. I became ill, physically ill, and was laid low for a few days, running a high temperature and in a condition of numbness. When the numbness passed, I was finished with the pact; it no longer existed. Fundamentally, I had made no decision. It had been made in me in some place I could not reach at all; I could do nothing about it. Or else it had taken me and put me in another place of extreme loneliness far away from the pact. Again I had firm ground under my feet, breathed freely, and felt as if I were in the wholesome, clean, serene cold of a starlit night. Nothing could seriously hurt me any more. A few days later, I picked up my papers and personal belongings at Rungstedlund without seeing the Baroness.

A short while after this conversation, Karen Blixen sent me a new "anecdote of destiny," "The Immortal Tale," which she previously had promised me, accompanied by a letter in which she wrote as if nothing had happened. It was near the end of

November, and some time later she asked me to come to visit
her. She was sick in bed, and we had tea in the bedroom at the
east end of the house; it was the first time I had ever set foot in
that room. I was quite taken by the low windowsills and the sea;
it was as if the water came right up below them. The room was
paneled with dark wood and reminded me of the interior of a
Norwegian mountain cottage. Even now she spoke as if the
conversation at Store Kro never had taken place; instead she
engrossed herself in my insoluble situation and expressed her
deep sympathy, and again I felt in a strange unreal way as if all
chronology had been suspended, as often happens with one's
memory when events are far in the past. The incident at Store
Kro faded into a bad dream, and I sat now as in convalescence
and heard her dark, familiar voice counseling me as well as it
could at this critical moment. She spoke of flying with Denys
Finch-Hatton: "In difficult or impossible situations later in life
I have often dreamt that I sat in Denys' plane, soaring high
above them, and that all possibilities were open, all the possibilities in the world as long as I soared, as long as I flew,
regardless of air pockets and vibrations. Couldn't you attempt
to feel yourself soaring, thinking that in reality all possibilities
are open to you? Could you not accept this uncertainty instead
of trying to force your way out of it come hell or high water?
Couldn't you avoid feeling obligated, torturing yourself to
make any decision whatever, but instead feel like a bird sitting
precariously on the outermost twig, forced to move and flutter
your wings all the time to prevent it from breaking under your
weight? Yes, couldn't you *ascend* if you had to?"

This comforting speech made the deepest impression on me;
it was like a healing balm that flowed out onto my wounded
soul, and when I took leave of her, she emanated nothing but
gentle authority and confidence and I felt completely understood and filled with the intense sweetness of homecoming.
And there really was something redeeming about the advice she

had given me. I followed it as well as I could, did not look far ahead, and trained myself not to reflect upon my life. I stayed at home and found in my work, whether scientific or poetic, the certainty and continuity I had lost.

The appearance of a new moon had always been a special event for Karen Blixen. When we were together, she never failed to point it out to me, but it had to be in the open air, not through glass, for that spelled bad luck. Consequently, she walked about diligently looking for it and she would call me outside when it came. She would then solemnly curtsy to it three times, and since she had very seriously bade me also to greet its arrival, I bowed three times. Therefore, when at the end of this year with its insurmountable difficulties, on a walk in the woods on New Year's Eve, I saw the new moon in the cold, dark blue air among the branches, I stopped, bowed three times as prescribed, and took it as an omen of a new beginning and a healing of our broken pact, and the next day I excitedly began a grateful letter to Karen Blixen with an appeal and a reference to the line from the play by Heiberg:

> Less than ever do I know what to do with the exter-
> nal circumstances that confront me and I am trying to
> adjust to the uncertainty, to rising, rising. How fortu-
> nate that I know you—that I have been allowed to meet
> you. Last night on New Year's Eve, I felt this strongly
> when suddenly—and not through a window—I saw
> the New Year's new moon, pure, sharp, and wonderful.
> I never see the new moon without thinking of you.

> Just a few words to let you know that Grete and I
> were in Jutland and celebrated Christmas there and the
> third day after Christmas have returned with Bo. How
> strongly I feel that he is my son, although I can't put
> that feeling into any kind of perspective. And that is
> precisely my problem: I cannot place things in their

proper relationship to one another without almost per-
ishing thereby. And so, as you said, I must *ascend*. . . .
   Now my pain is never the pain of being outside, but
the pain of being involved, sucked up. Whatever the
circumstances, I am deeply grateful. You have taught
me much, more than may be discerned from my continuing foolishness. You have taught me an immeasurable
amount. You are my refuge, the clean wild calm in the
eye of the storm. You have robed yourself wonderfully,
or God has, for the feast of life. May I, now and then,
have responded.

When in January I next visited Karen Blixen, it was with
great expectation and renewed trust. Once again the visit
turned out to be exactly the opposite of what I had expected, at
least in the beginning. To be sure, Store Kro still was not
mentioned, but she now held against me my lack of seriousness
concerning the pact and once more she put before me a letter,
this time one of my letters to her from January 1950. "Your
letter of promise," she named it, "the one that gave impetus to
the pact between us. And now, just two years later, I trust you
can see how badly you have failed, how little the pact means to
you and speaks to you. And now I would like to know whether
or not you will become serious about it. You must decide now
because it cannot work in this manner. It cannot continue this
way." I was caught completely off guard having to make decisions about something that I believed to have been settled after
our last visit, namely, the pact, in spite of everything, in spite of
the grotesque and nightmarish interlude, in spite of her notice
and my giving it up: something that still existed, as if by divine
inertia, by decisions over our heads, so to speak. As it previously
had been up to me to cancel it, so it was now up to me to confirm
it, if not to re-create it outright, and no more than I had previously been able to do the former was I now able to do the latter. I

did not know how I had failed until I was told, and when I was told, the telling did not include how to avoid failure in the future when I had to live my own life and be the person I was. In short, I had no idea how I should go about taking the pact more seriously than I had done so far. In the acute perplexity of the moment, I spontaneously reverted to the decision I made sometime between the conversation at Store Kro and my last visit to Rungstedlund, and I started to say that it was impossible to take seriously something that did not exist anymore, but she interrupted me: "No, don't say anything now, but think it over carefully before you answer and then write to me. But don't wait too long."

Then she asked me to play a record, first the andante of Haydn's string quartet No. 17 and then Schubert's "Faith in Spring" (*Frühlingsglaube*), which we used to play whenever a gloomy mood had to be dispelled and we needed to be cheered up. When the music was over, she suddenly said with her special blend of authority and irresistible roguishness: "What's wrong is that I am not twenty-five years younger. If I were, we could take a two-week trip to Venice and straighten things out. Then there would not be so much to talk about." And with that she launched into jokes and plans about the most remote things and immediate ones as well, namely, the following day's luncheon party with "her daughters" that I have already described.

On that occasion she spoke of the Erlking (*Erlkönig*). She identified with him and mocked the stupid boy who was frightened, unable to accept anything and who "just whined and thought he was going to die." There was no question who the stupid boy was. Later she played the "*Erlkönig*" and when she had closed the lid of the record player, she said, "We really wear masks as we grow older, the masks of our age, but the young do not know that or do not think of them as masks when they are with us. They think we are the way we look. But that is not at all the case. It is often a great relief and release for me, without the presence of younger people, to be together with persons of my own age and to enjoy myself and laugh with them because we know we wear masks and we can forget them." She was silent for a moment, but did not seem quite satisfied. It was obvious she wanted to get hold of something more tenable than the being behind the mask, something more tangible and indestructible, demonstrable and indisputable, and with her characteristic consistency she finally said with romantic flourish and almost with triumph, "But one thing is certain and that I know: I shall become a perfect, an exceptionally beautiful, skeleton and I am looking forward to that." She smiled her wry, cryptic smile and not for one second did I doubt that indeed she was looking forward to it, that she did not have to be satisfied sadly to look back at former beauty, but, even expectantly, could look ahead to a beauty to be. She then played a joyful concerto for flute by Handel and gave herself up to listening with a blissful expression on her face, as if her skeleton in the fullness of time perhaps also could be taken apart in its bony framework and recomposed into pipes on which could be played divine and earthly music. It turned out to be a very enjoyable evening, almost like one of the evenings we had had in the spring before I left for Bonn.

When I got home after the successful luncheon with the freesias in my hair, I was in high spirits and far from pondering her serious question. On the days that followed when the question posed itself again with renewed strength, I was no closer to an answer. The impulse to decide and the answer, instilled in me spontaneously by the New Year's new moon, had been canceled by our last conversation and I had now set the deadline on my birthday, February 2, 1952. On that day I received greetings and a large bouquet of hyacinths from Rungstedlund, but as I still did not know what to answer, and, moreover, was sick, I just wrote a short note of thanks. Gradually, subconsciously, and later consciously, as I extended the teachings about the accepted uncertainty to cover also my relationship with Karen Blixen—and why should it not be applicable there also?—it turned out to be a powerful, productive incentive. The distraction caused by the conflict ceased to exist and suppressed creative powers were set free. I shelved the work on my dissertation and began to write poetry; more and more I felt the word as my only refuge other than my son who was then five years old. I loved to read fairy tales to him, and through them I understood life better than through anything else. Between the first and the tenth of February I wrote "The Sorcerers on Troll Skerry" (*Sejdmaendene paa Skratteskaer*), and with this poem and "The House of Childhood" I felt I had the caissons on which to build a new poetic bridge, extreme expressions of pain and happiness respectively, the one created about the time the pact had been reinforced and consolidated, the other about the time it was dissolved and set aside.

On the seventeenth of March, while I was in Copenhagen, Karen Blixen came to pay me a visit at Sletten. As I had not yet seen her since our conversation in January, I wrote to her the following day:

> It is too bad I was not in when you and Pasop came
> to see me. It may seem strange to you that you have
> neither heard from me nor seen me for so long. It is
> simply because I do not have the strength; that has
> happened many times before and it made no difference.
> But after our last conversation the situation has changed;
> now it does make a difference. The New Year's new
> moon has meant to me, among other things, that I have
> had to stay away from Rungstedlund at least until I
> have answered you. I prefer to put it in writing and I
> have not felt able to do that either. I have had a string
> of visitations of all sorts of minor infirmities, but apart
> from those I am well; I take occasional long walks and

now and then experience a clearing of the mind and a
spell on wings. Each time usually for too short a time.
These are just tentative remarks until I gather strength
to discuss the matter in depth.

I think that I was in better shape than the letter indicates; at
least, that is how I remember it and I can also tell by the hand-
writing. Just after completing my poem "The Sorcerers on Troll
Skerry," I had hit my head on a door frame in the low-ceilinged
house of a friend and was down with a new slight concussion.
But in spite of various physical and mental incapacities, I was
fundamentally all right and in the process of finding my bal-
ance. I was still writing poetry and did not want to be disturbed; and as far as the pact and the answer about it were
concerned, I knew precisely that if I did not continue to accept
uncertainty, but insisted on reaching a decision, I would in-
evitably run into the granite of certainty: that the pact was
finished.

On the seventeenth of May, exactly two months later, Karen
Blixen again paid us a visit and invited me to go to Stockholm
with her to see the *Oresteia*. She thought it might call forth
latent dramatic talents she assumed I possessed, something she
already had hinted at with regard to Shakespeare's plays and
something she considered more likely to open me up to the
world than my exclusive immersion in lyric poetry. Again she
wanted me out of the nest and what she found to be my frustrating idyll—and exposed to the shock it would be to see this great
tragic trilogy. Truly the thought fascinated me, but as usual she
gave me time to consider, and as soon as she had left I knew I
would not go with her, that going along would be on false
premises. When my wife reminded me that I had promised to
deliver an article to *Heretica* within two weeks, I made use of the
promise with cool and ill-concealed relief the next day to write
her a note of regret. The reference to the promise had the effect

of a highly transparent excuse. I could easily have gone along, and the article was never written anyway. In a short letter she now urged me, in the name of Nietzsche, to say yes instead of persistently answering no, and understandably she became very bitter when I stubbornly repeated my refusal.

In the meantime, during this period of uncertainty, various decisions had been reached. My friend, who had no children, made up her mind to get a divorce, and I decided to stay with my marriage, not just because I had a child, reason enough in itself, but because I had no choice whatever as I understood things. It came about in the following manner.

Karen Blixen wanted me to excel and to separate myself from middle-class society, if in no other way, by doing something inadmissible, committing some sort of crime, so that I would be relegated from the social context and become dependent on her for protection in my conspiracy. "Whatever you do that is condemned by everyone else," she said, "you can calmly rely on me and rest assured that I will be on your side." She returned to the subject often and, to reassure me how deeply serious she was about it, she once gave me a long, slender silver letter opener with the claw of a lion she had shot in Africa mounted in gold and attached as a small handle. On the blade was the inscription, "I am on your side." (I lost it on the trip to Norway, and it was never returned.)

She clearly did not mean a petty crime. It had to be a crime of sublime intent and motive. It had to possess meaning in another and more comprehensive context than the one it violated; to serve and be of a higher moral order, it had to be a violation to fulfill a deeper, more fundamental law, like the law of nature instead of those of social conventions. As an example, Karen Blixen told me of a native woman in Africa who lived with a husband whose behavior was brutal and criminal and how she had helped this woman kill him by inducing him to fall and break his neck. It had been done by magic, and Karen Blixen told me the story to exemplify the ruthlessness she thought might be required to serve the cause of the true good. She regretted that something similar could not be done and was impossible in our civilized middle-class society and that, if it came to such a test, she did not think she had the strength and the nerve required.

If she had had that strength or if we had lived in other times or in another kind of society, I do not think Karen Blixen would have hesitated long in getting my wife out of the way. Not because my wife was a bad person or a criminal, but because she interfered with the purpose of my life, which was to give that life its highest artistic expression under the aegis of Karen Blixen. As it was, she had to be content with simply wishing, and one thing is certain: Karen Blixen wished that my wife not exist and she wished it to such a degree that by this intense, perceptible wish alone and the authority and knowledge of what was best for me that it represented, my wife felt threatened, her very existence called into question. Intoxicated by Rilke's metaphysical treatment of death, which I, although an avid reader of Rilke, had never taken seriously, and by the fascinating resonance of death in Schubert's "The Maid of the Mill" (*Die Schöne Müllerin*) and *Die Winterreise*, which we played constantly at the time, my wife went to the brink of suicide. Her suicide attempt, which took place while I was in Norway, was foiled in the nick of time. When my wife told me what she had intended to do, I was shocked and filled with conflicting feelings, a deep and painful guilt and a dull and inarticulate indignation. The intent alone, and the possibility that the attempt might have succeeded, paralyzed, for years thereafter, any effort to break up and leave. It could also be said that it relieved me and canceled any doubt about what I should do. After that I did experience many happy moments in my marriage, although it was doomed in the long run, doomed precisely by what kept it together, the lack of freedom.

A few days after my wife's suicide attempt, my friend went abroad. Perhaps there was an element of conjuring in her departure, a wild hope that we would see each other again and the persistent, uncertain hope for a miracle that I could not exorcise either. The parting was final nevertheless, and after I had escorted her to the train and said good-bye, I did not understand how I continued to function; it was as if someone else moved in my body and made it stand up and walk. When I got home, I finally knew how I had to answer Karen Blixen. On the fourth of June I wrote to her:

> Now I shall try to answer a question that since January I have been unable to answer with a yes or a no. . . .
> When at Store Kro in November you asked for your release and requested me to give notice of my cancellation of the pact, which only I could give after what had happened in Brittany, I asked for time to consider the matter. Only once before in my life have I wished that someone would keep her ties to me against her will. Nothing came of that, nor will it in this case. I therefore renounce the pact and release you.

One thing that I did not understand and that made me very angry was that Karen Blixen had told other people of my secret love. This had given my friend and me quite a shock because she was the only one entrusted with the knowledge and no one else knew about it because she had insisted that it should be that way. The following part of my letter refers to this. I take the sole responsibility for confiding in her because my friend had promised not even to tell me that she had told her:

You wrote to me in Bonn that if I ever fell in love it was my duty to tell you; you would later explain why. For this reason alone I told you what had happened. I could not know beforehand that it was such a terrible mistake to tell you, but I see now that it was. . . .

Dear Baroness, you have said yourself that the best thing about this affair is that no one knows about it. Let that remain the best thing about the affair, I beseech you.

You have stated several times that you did not understand what made me so sad in Bonn. Now I believe I know: It was the first time in my life that I experienced perfect solitude. I am experiencing that solitude now and it is often hard. I go my own way in it, but it gives me one reward: all my fears and concerns are transformed into pain and in the pain *"wiederhole ich das Glück"* (I repeat the happiness), as Goethe says. . . .

At one point or another, dear Baroness, you are on my side; that I still believe and I keep the letter opener as a pledge. But in reality we cannot go on together. The most exalted and most beautiful things that I have experienced with you I shall remember with gratitude till the end of my days.

This time I thought that the matter had been settled once and for all, but I was mistaken as usual. Karen Blixen answered promptly: "I have as much faith in you as I ever had. You do me an injustice in your letter." Shortly afterward she telephoned and said that we could not terminate our friendship in this way and that she also had the right to a reply. Because there were several things that she wanted to say to me, I had to visit her. We agreed on a date, and for the first time in almost half a year we saw each other again at Rungstedlund. For the first time since it had occurred, she mentioned the conversation at Store

Kro. She said that she had been terribly excited but that she had not really meant what she said—that I should not take it seriously—and asked me to forgive her. This took me as much by surprise as her remarks originally had. I could not comprehend how something I had accepted seriously and with so much pain was not meant after all. If I had not been made a fool of, I at least felt a bit like a fool and I could not regroup the forces I had committed to accept and live with the rupture. I did not know what to believe and said so.

To this Karen Blixen replied that evidently stronger means were required and that she wanted us to renew the pact and permanently confirm it by the mingling of our blood. Blood was the strongest and most powerful bond between people, she said, and a pact confirmed by blood would constitute an unbreakable covenant. "Blood is stronger than words," she said. Considering the tremendous tensions that existed between us, I thought it better to keep it revocable, that it probably would be best if we got together without any formal pact so that we could be together in friendliness and perhaps feel our meeting to be a plus instead of, as it now was, a continuing minus of mutual betrayal. But because I felt that it was embarrassing to answer her strong proposal in such a way and because I did not know quite how to formulate my response, I decided to wait, and my hesitation was made easier because Karen Blixen had already gone on to the next subject while I was thinking. She usually did so when she felt that nothing worthwhile would come from the pause.

The poet Jørgen Gustava Brandt was one of my younger friends and collaborators at *Heretica*. He was enraptured by Karen Blixen and had a special understanding of her work. I introduced him to her just before I left for Bonn because I thought that they would enjoy each other. Gustava thereafter began to come to Rungstedlund and a relationship developed between him and the Baroness, fundamentally different from hers and mine because he and I were so vastly different. He possessed much intuition, founded perhaps on an unprejudiced and almost unselfish curiosity, resulting in a completely relaxed and even-tempered cynicism that contrasted oddly with his youth. He had a kind of exceptionally well-developed mental olfactory sense; when he entered a room he could be seen virtually to sniff it out—as if he instinctively and carefully registered the emanation from every bit of a sentence, every possession or thing in the room. Like a cat, he knew immediately with his whole being whether he felt well or bad where he was. He also knew how others felt, and if he felt fine himself he spared no effort to make whomever he was with feel fine also. He had none of the self-centered quality of youth; he was beyond it and regarded it as an incomprehensible excess of which he knew the outcome beforehand. "He has never been young," said Karen Blixen when she got to know him. "He skipped his youth." To top it off, he dressed and carried himself with a pompous, meticulous vanity and with a style unrelated to anything else. But Karen Blixen delighted in it and had her own humorous explanation, as it appears from this letter I received in Bonn:

Your friend Jørgen Gustava Brandt has twice paid me a visit. It was pleasant to talk with him. Clara and I agree that he looks like one of the mannequins you see in a haberdashery and when he leaves at night we imagine that he goes directly to the English House to stand there when they open the shop in the morning. We imagine him in the different positions he takes up as the shop's salespeople dress him in a new suit, his face always wearing the same concentrated, fiercely staring look. It is fun for me to be with him because he is so well versed in older Danish literature. He has written a short essay, "Two Siblings" (*To Søskende*), in which he compares Goldschmidt* and me, and in his peculiar approach as an amateur of literature he also thinks he finds points of similarity between me and Wessel.†

After that Karen Blixen often referred to Brandt as "English House." When she met him she was working on one of her "anecdotes of destiny," "The Immortal Story," and as she got to know him better, she found in him a kind of model for the clerk in the story, and both the clerk and Brandt came to be called Elishama. I believe that what in particular attracted Karen Blixen to him was a kind of originality which is neither usual nor normally thought of in connection with the word, namely intellectual originality. It sounds like a contradiction because originality instinctively gets connected with feelings, but intellectual originality does exist and this is the specific trait the model and the character in "The Immortal Story" have in common. It may have contributed to make the relationship between him and Karen Blixen much less complicated and more relaxed than the one between her and me. Because they got to know each other during and after my sojourn in Bonn, just at the time our relationship became more tense and confused, I think it was quite relaxing for her to be with him. It was especially relaxing also because he was totally unimpressed by being with her and at times even flippant. As is said of the clerk in "The Immortal Story," in a certain sense he was utterly shameless. "Can't you see that she is a vamp from the twenties," Gustava had said with a grin on one occasion. I could see what he meant when she wore

---

*Meïr Aron Goldschmidt (1819–1887), short-story writer and novelist, editor of the witty radical journal *Corsair* (1840). A master of style, he ranks among the great novelists of Denmark. —Tr.

†Johan Herman Wessel (1742–1785), Dano-Norwegian poet, humorist, and playwright, a master of parody. —Tr.

a cloche hat and with her bare arms looked particularly outlandish and sophisticated, but not otherwise. To me she was and remained the Pellegrina of her story.

As I became more and more hopelessly entangled in my situation and as my isolation became increasingly inaccessible to all encouragement and enchantment, Pellegrina undoubtedly needed precisely what diversion and amusement she could derive from Gustava. The culmination must have come about mid-September, for at that time I received the following postcard from him:

> The other day at Rungstedlund we spoke about laughter and tears. We finally made certain decisions— the Baroness had a good idea. Together we'll now establish the circus "Gustava." My job is to be the clown and the Baroness will be the cashier. She will also help me write comic monologues. We shall put on our first show in Bonn as soon as possible. Perhaps Adenauer will be our patron. When it is time to make reservations, we'll drop you a line. Heil!
>
> GUSTAVA

To this day I don't really understand what purpose the postcard served or what its significance was. Gustava was one of those to whom Karen Blixen had betrayed our trust, to what extent I could not know, but the magnitude of the insult, which in this case had been added to bitter injury, he had surely not been aware of. If he had, he would hardly have written the postcard. No, I had no doubt that someone had guided his hand. Was it not as if our love was observed from Olympian orchestra seats, as if we were a clumsy pastoral couple greeted with a roar of laughter? Was it not also an act of vengeance for offenses I unknowingly or unavoidably had inflicted on her? In any case I wrote to her:

I have failed in many things, but this I have not
deserved. In my eyes this is the sort of petty demoniac
behavior you detest. . . .
I think this means that we shall no longer see each
other. You do not understand me; I do not understand
you. Why do each other more harm and postpone what
apparently cannot be averted?

How we got together again I neither understand nor remember; I only recall that she disclaimed any and all responsibility
for the postcard. I did not believe it, but let it pass because
either way she withdrew her insult and she now showed her
change of heart by supporting, contrary to all expectations, my
absent friend and me. She promised us all the support I once had
believed in and had counted on. "Never forget," she said, "that
you must hope against hope and believe against belief." On
other occasions she asked again and again: "Is there really nothing I can help you with? Nothing at all?" I answered no because
I considered the case closed. "Could I help you with something
else?" I became somewhat confused, thanked her for her readiness to help, and answered that I really did not need any assistance, that I thought everything was going well and that I
had no complaints.

That was both true and false. It was a relief that a decision
had been reached and carried out, that a course had been shaped,
but I also despaired that it was almost beyond my power to stay
with my marriage after what had happened. Yet I had no illu-
sions; it was also beyond my power to walk out. Karen Blixen
saw through the situation and complained bitterly, "You *will*
not accept help. You are of a titanic nature, you will accept help
neither from the supernatural powers nor from me. You will
leave nothing to the gods, you will not let them make decisions
nor offer you gifts. You will accept nothing, just be defiant."
With a reference to my poem "The House of Childhood" she

called me an Atlas; a section of the poem has the Atlas figure as
the central metaphor and is about titanic rage and desperation.
Somber but teasing, she quoted from a poem by Heine, which I
did not know, "I Wretched Atlas" (*Ich unglücksel'ger Atlas*):

> Du wolltest glücklich sein, unendlich glücklich
> Oder unendlich elend, stolzes Herz,
> Und jetzo bist du elend.
>
> (You wanted to be happy, infinitely happy
> or infinitely wretched, proud heart,
> and now you are wretched.)

The lines struck home. For the first time I thought that I
understood Heine, although I was not under twenty or over
forty, as Karen Blixen had said one had to be in order to understand him. I said this was as good as a poem by Goethe, and she
knew that I could not rate any poem higher. Apart from that I
had nothing to add. There was much truth in the diagnosis and
she realized that it had found its mark. Later she accused me of
siding with the superhuman, the stubborn and defiant, who
would have no part of grace and play and mercy, of *la grâce de
Dieu*, while she sided with the divine who floated and swam in
this element, and she said, "Could you not be on the side of the
gods like me? In return, perhaps some day they will be on your
side and will support and guide you."

Another time when I visited her, she walked about, restless
and dejected, before the fireplace while she talked. "You are
better than I am, that is the problem," she said. "The difference
between us is that you have an immortal soul and I do not have
one. It is the same with mermaids or nixies, they do not have
one either. They live longer than those with immortal souls, but
when they die they disappear totally and without a trace. But
who can entertain and please and transport people better than
the nixie when she is present, when she plays and enchants and
makes people dance more wildly and love more ardently than

they normally do?" "Look," she said finally, pointing to a small puddle of rainwater that had penetrated the leaky windows, "she will disappear and all that she leaves behind is a streak of water along the floor."

This, the third period after the rupture, was like a very protracted swan song or one of Beethoven's endless finales. Because nothing that came from Karen Blixen interfered with my life any longer, our conversations were more repetitious and it is difficult to place them in chronological order, with the exception of a few that stand out in their abysmal bitterness or halcyon clarity. When the latter occurred, I could, as if carried by a mighty wave, once again be in the lost paradise under the old spell. Then I would again sit in the green room at a festive table, empty my bottle of red wine and my piglet-shaped bottle of cognac and give myself up completely to companionship. Everything was as it once was except that Karen Blixen now always wore long and strikingly beautiful and elegant evening dresses. Shortly after one such successful visit, on November 21, 1952, I received a new invitation:

Dear Magister,

I was very glad to see you here the other day. Would you consider giving me the pleasure of your company for dinner Thursday or Friday of next week? Clara is in Copenhagen; so I am alone and need a bit of conversation.

Let me know if you will stay the night. If not, I will get a taxi to take you home. I have reached the age when I cannot have clockwatchers as guests.

I replied that I would come and that I preferred to stay the night. When I arrived and stepped into the green room, she rose, came over and embraced me, and said with remarkable but suppressed emotion in her voice, "*Sei mir gegrüsst, sei mir geküsst*" (Let me greet you, let me kiss you), a greeting she had used in the past when she was particularly happy to see me, as, for example, in Paris, but never before with such feeling. It was based on the opening lines of Schubert's wonderful song which I had heard for the first time on her old gramophone. It turned into a long and unusual evening.

It was as if our sorrows were all ancient, the most recent of mine as old as the oldest of hers, as if under the pressure of the immense space of time they had become nameless and shapeless and now mixed like oil and nourished the moment's bonfire. I drank white and red wine as well as the final cognac, and as I grew more and more intoxicated we both swung between contemplative profundity and light-headed gaiety. I was completely indifferent to what had happened and what might possibly happen in the future.

Suddenly she got up from the table and left the room slowly, without a word. She came back a little later with a revolver in her hand. She positioned herself with one hand resting on her high-backed chair, and raising the revolver in the other hand, drew a bead on me, and kept it for a long time. I was not in the least astonished; nothing could disturb my perfect happiness. Everything, I thought, is insoluble: you can never be happier than you are now and so it may as well be now as later. She looked steadily at me and I at her with a mutual, mad understanding. Then she slowly brought down her arm and went back out the door. She came back a little later, sat down, and began to talk as if nothing had happened.

We continued to talk until very late. When I went to bed, she put Tschaikovsky's *Andante Cantabile* on the record player while I lay listening, unbelievably, blissfully intoxicated, risen, so to speak, above myself. I remember nothing of what we talked about that evening, only her salutation, the music, and the one magic movement of her arm as she raised the revolver. Neither of us ever said a single word afterward about that occasion.

A bit later, just before Christmas, Karen Blixen sent me at Sletten some artificial fruit and her story "Babette's Feast," which was finally in print. I answered with the letter about celebrating Christmas in the bosom of my family, at the top of which she had made the notation: IDIOT.

THE CLOAK TRILOGY 〜〜〜〜

TO UNDERSTAND what had happened to me, I needed an external solitude that corresponded to my internal loneliness. I found it in my summer cottage at Kandestederne, a small, thick-walled cinder-block house located on a dune by the ocean, several kilometers from the nearest neighbor in an uninhabited stretch of dunes, a bit of wild nature by Danish standards and one of the few places in the country where that still exists. As things stood, it was a place after my own heart and one that I really came to appreciate for the first time. I moved in, and in the following years lived there alone for three months in the spring and three months in the fall. I read and wrote and roamed about the countryside along the North Sea.

During the entire year of 1953, the third year since the pact had been established, Karen Blixen and I saw very little of each other. I suppose that we both had plenty to do trying to make out what had happened to us, and both of us worked hard. She worked on the stories for the projected novel *Albondocani* and on her *Baaltale* (Oration at a Bonfire, Fourteen Years Late). I worked on my dissertation and on poetry, a cantata for the university of Aarhus, and translations of works by Hölderlin. By their extraordinary complexity, my personal experiences had become a kind of taboo; while I remained too close to them, I could not transform them into poetry. I turned instead to Hölderlin, in whose love story I found something similar to my own. Through the translation of "The Parting" (*Der Abschied*) and "Menon's Dirge for Diotima" (*Menons Klagen um Diotima*), I found an outlet for the sorrow that still welled up like a dark, low pressure within me. Together with other translations of Hölderlin's poems, they were published in the September 1953 issue of *Heretica*. With the exception of two short poems, Hölderlin had not previously been translated into Danish. On October 4, Karen Blixen wrote to me:

> I want to thank you for your translations of Hölderlin in *Heretica*.
>
> I cannot find words to tell you how the poems have moved me—mightily, with pain and great joy, a bow was touched to all the strings in me. It was like the waves of old times. *Quel bonheur, quel bonheur!* I have not slept, but it was a lovely night. I can still feel the resonance strongly about me, and I rush to write to you (I am having guests for lunch).

It was as if Karen Blixen had now really taken a different view of my love affair and had disavowed her jealous rejection of it. Not that she denied it outright, but now she transformed it objectively. She fantasied about the events, about what had happened and what possibly could happen, in a trilogy of stories that she gave me to read that same autumn. The trilogy consisted of the three chapters from the novel *Albondocani*: "The Cloak," "Night Walk," and "Of Secret Thoughts and of Heaven." The degree of fantasy with which a real-life situation and the persons in it are treated is, of course, of utmost importance. With Karen Blixen, the heat of fantasy is at the melting point, and furthermore, she projects the persons into supernatural size and strangeness as archetypes—quite the contrary of what she does in the tale "Echoes," where her procedure is more like a diminution.

In "The Cloak," the very name of the aging sculptor, Leonidas Allori, indicates her poetic identification with him: a sublime embodiment and revelation of her animus and an allusion to her totem animal, the lion, which is also the name of the singer in the tale "The Dreamers," Pellegrina Leoni. At the very beginning of the tale, he is called "the Lion of the Mountains."

His favorite pupil and disciple—and Karen Blixen, in a way, regarded me as hers, as is evident also in "Echoes," the tale that continues "The Dreamers"—falls in love with the master's young wife. After futile resistance, she promises him to give herself fully to him, and they plan to meet while she is in the mountains and the old master is in prison, awaiting a death sentence. But the old man comes to the meeting in the cloak borrowed from his disciple, who as a hostage remains in the cell the night before the master's execution at dawn. Through this romantic plot, remote in time and space, Karen Blixen's reflections over the events and the nature of jealousy found simultaneously labyrinthine experimentation and passionately straightforward expression. It is like a fire that leaps from person to person, unchangeable in itself, but consuming in different ways: raw and elementary in the case of the young man, with red smoky flames, through the shimmering heat of which he watches the embrace of the two the last night and is haunted by fantasies of killing, remorse, and shame. On the other hand, the old man is consumed by a fine, clear glow. An infinite sublimation takes place and culminates in an inscrutable identification with the revenge of the master on the young disciple and in forgiveness of him sprung from an exalted fatherly sentiment and a triumphant understanding and acceptance of love's transfiguration.

Although it is removed in fantasy just as far from the actual events, the next tale, "Night Walk," also receives its watermark and its signature from them. Its theme is the total insomnia that indeed afflicted me at that time, and with which Karen Blixen was well acquainted; and an ingenious deciphering of its psychic causes is intoned in these words: "Will the narrator be believed by such people as have themselves experience of sleeplessness, when he tells them that from the beginning this affliction was the victim's own choice?" This is what happened to the faithless disciple after his master's death, and as he now will be together only with people who are awake and keep watch, it would be natural for him to be together with the deceased's other pupils, "but on no account would he join them, for they would be talking of Leonidas Allori and would greet him as the chosen disciple upon whom the eye of the master had last dwelt. Yes, he thought, and laughed, as if I were Elisha, the follower of the great prophet Elijah, on whom the passenger in the chariot of fire threw his mantle!" This is the signature, the reference to the pact, the covenant that Karen Blixen established between us with words from the same biblical passage so that I should make no mistake about it. And according to the directions of the fortune teller, the person to whom insomnia and sleepwalking lead the sleepless is the archetype of the faithless and of traitors: Judas.

The third tale of the trilogy, "Of Secret Thoughts and of Heaven," is a brilliant, lingering epilogue, an unexpected happy ending. The much desired happiness has arrived, the lovers are united, how we are not told, and live a heavenly mature family life with children and fame. Under these fundamentally changed and happy circumstances, he is paid a visit by the philosopher and puppet-show manager, Pizzuti, whom he had met and confided in shortly after he had decided not to sleep any more. The tale centers on their conversation about what has happened to them since they met long ago—the husband's doubt whether Leonidas really knew of his treachery—and of what will happen to them after death: a conversation on secrets and on heaven.

It was with an extremely maternal gesture, characteristic of her generous and zealous, magnificent and fervent nature, that Karen Blixen had given me the tales to read and had allowed me to understand that I should interpret the last one of the trilogy not only as a fictitious postscript to the other two but also a prediction and thereby as a magically reinforced hope of what eventually might become my story, my story as she wanted it to be. For I believe that with one segment of her feelings and with the stronger part of herself she wanted it to end in clarification and gaiety.

THE PARTING

ON TWELFTH NIGHT, 1954, I dined again at Rungstedlund. As usual, I was the only guest, and Karen Blixen, derisive and gay, was not wearing the accustomed evening dress but rather a Pierrot costume. Since we were last together, she told me, she had been to Jutland and had visited my friend, who had recently returned to Denmark, but my friend had kept quiet about everything and had scarcely answered any question. Later she had refused to receive visitors and had written to the Baroness that she wanted to be left in peace. This evening began to resemble, more than anything, a bitter satirical play. Karen Blixen had again changed her attitude, and now poked fun at my friend, whom I still did not see, and at me because I did not do something about the relationship. But considering what we were like, that did not astonish her: "You with your foolish recalcitrance and cowardice, you, who dare not mingle your blood with another's simply because you're afraid of the sight of blood, and, as for her, don't you see that her soul is no bigger than a pea?" I got quite worked up, but was so taken by surprise that I was totally paralyzed. And she went on with such monstrous jokes about us, about everything and everybody, that I, much against my will, had to laugh and let myself get carried along in a whirl of wild, hilarious, terrible irony; no one looked normal, and no one escaped. It was the perfect nihilism or black mass, and in one way or another it did liberate something suppressed in me, so that I ended up participating instead of protesting.

She suddenly became serious and said, "But I'm always the one who has gone about thinking of you and what I could do for you. Now cross your heart and answer: Have you thought of anything but your own misfortune? Have you ever really thought of me, how I was and what you could do for me?" And what answer could I give? It would have been ridiculous to have answered yes and enumerated how, and comical to have answered: No, come to think of it—I have not, or, frankly, I have forgotten. And there was something to her accusations: when one is unhappy one thinks mostly of oneself. So I said nothing, and no words were necessary either. She proceeded to go into detail with an intensity that had the character of a curse. And Karen Blixen truly possessed the ability to curse. What happens to the one subjected to such a curse? As far as I can see, what happens, psychologically at least, is this: the one who curses brings to light everything notoriously dubious in the one attacked, everything bad and inferior and pitiable, and turns it into the principal being, belittles and suppresses everything positive, and then insinuates that this agitated scum, this scarecrow, is, plain and simple, the person cursed. This is exactly how Karen Blixen proceeded, after which she swept up what remained of me with an inexpressibly tender gesture, and put me to bed.

That was the last time I visited Karen Blixen at Rungstedlund. In the days that followed, I suffered a severe mental hangover, first and foremost because of the diabolically ironic and sardonically humoristic excesses, which I felt had had a debilitating effect, not the least when they, as in this case, joined with the curse's total reduction of my person to form a strong chemical compound. For one horrible moment, I felt as if I really, without knowing it but by no means innocently, had accepted her invitation of long standing and had mounted her broomstick with her.

That night Karen Blixen had induced me to deny everything, including my love. Slowly it dawned on me that, wearing different masks, she inscrutably and consistently had opposed and sabotaged the relationship between my friend and me so that it should not reach its consummation *and* that it should not be understood as tragic. I believe that deep down she was set against its attaining any kind of validity, and the last decisive clash between us was fought on this point. That was why my affair was denied consummation by moral indignation, and its tragic aspect denied by ridicule. She demanded therefore tragedy when I sought fulfillment, and fulfillment when I accepted the tragic—and in both cases maintained that we failed the laws of history, the history of which we were part. Our relationship was not permitted to exist, nor even *to have existed*. And her notion of my taking on a snake charmer meant that I should find someone by whom I could be sensually but not spiritually satisfied. Only one person could give me that spiritual satisfaction: the one I was bound to by the pact.

I realized that not just the pact but the whole friendship it stood for had to come to an end: we had gone too far to keep it alive. After weeks of pondering the situation, I wrote a long letter without any conclusion, and I did not mail it because I now knew from experience that it would probably only lead to new conversations. I decided therefore just to withdraw without a word of explanation; to come up with excuses no matter how transparent they were (for that she had schooled me well) and to stay away.

My evasions and excuses, although they made her as bitterly angry as my forthright refusals, produced the desired result: she declared that she no longer wanted to see me at Rungstedlund. When she changed her mind and wanted to see me after all, she called me to meet her at the Nivaa, a stream about nineteen miles north of Copenhagen, partly because she would not retract her expulsion of me, and partly, perhaps, because she felt I could not bring myself to refuse her when she was ready to meet me halfway. "It is a place fit for you to meet the Nixie."

Another time we met on Ewald's Hill; she asked me to approach it from the Rungsted road, apparently because she did not want anybody in the house to know of our meeting. Accordingly, I walked from the road across the fields to the hill. It was a

THE PARTING · 147

quiet, sunny afternoon, and there she sat on the bench waiting for me with Pasop. Karen Blixen greeted me amicably and bade me to sit down. I felt warm and glad to see her again in this familiar spot, where we had sat together so many times. She asked what had happened with my friend and me. When in the course of the conversation she came to the sad course of events and said that she always had wanted the best for the two of us and had supported us from the beginning and that she did not understand my grudge, I became indignant and objected, against my inclination not to do so. It seemed to me that whatever I did it would be wrong and would give me a bad conscience, but I chose, nevertheless, not to withhold a protest that had to come out sooner or later. That made her equally indignant and she said: "Yes, but are you really so full of spite and resentment and thirst for revenge that we never shall be able to get on?" I answered positively that I would very much like to get on, but that I simply could not when she herself picked up the subject and changed the facts so that I could not recognize them at all. "I feel," I said, "that our conversations lately have degenerated into a fight about who will decide what has taken place, and if I give in, you will, in the future, derive no joy whatever from being together with me, and I cannot come only 'for pleasure,' as you explicitly wish." "For pleasure" was a quotation from Shelley's "Song" ("Rarely, rarely comest thou"), which she had used often to emphasize that I should come according to my own inclinations, only for the sake of my own enjoyment and never "for pity," as the poem also states. I concluded by invoking a participant in one of our imaginary symposia: "If I have to explain myself at all, I can do it best in the words of Goethe (words condensed or that I can no longer locate):

> Liegt dir Gestern klar und offen
> Kannst du Morgen wieder hoffen

(If yesterday is clear and open to you,
you can hope again tomorrow)

and if you want to call it spite and resentment that I would very
much like to see yesterday in a clarity that is clear to both of us,
go ahead and do so."

She flared up and said that I was and remained a resentful and
petty person who understood nothing and who was willing to
ruin everything for so little, just as I had done after the incident
at Store Kro, and how bitterly disappointing it was when she
thought of how much she had hoped for and expected of me:
"But that was of course in the days when I thought you would
become a great poet," she concluded with biting disdain. The
whole thing was so unalterably sad that I cut it short by saying
finally that she should no more occupy herself with and worry
about my future than she should determine my past. "Nothing
is farther from me," she said and added, apparently illogically,
but in reality in line with her own sovereign logic, "When I met
you I did not even know you were married." She had said that
before, and what answer should I give? For a moment I thought
of saying that it would have sounded funny, but that right away
at our first meeting I should have said, "How do you do, my
name is ———, and I am married," but I kept the imperti-
nence to myself. We were already deep into a quarrel in which
the conversation simply rotates and is trivialized by reflexlike
repetitions. Both of us must have felt it, for we suddenly parted
in somber bitterness, barely saying good-bye. Once again I
thought it was our last meeting. But the finale was longer than I
could have imagined; there followed a painful postlude. The
events were repeated in the same pattern, but with a change of
place.

Late one morning in September 1954 while I sat working in my
cottage on the North Sea, there was suddenly a knock on the

windowpane behind my back. I turned around, and there outside stood Karen Blixen motioning to me. I rushed to open the
door. She shook hands and said, "I have traveled up through
Jutland and have walked all the way out here just to visit you, to
see how you are and how you are getting on. Here I am; may I
come in?" I was unshaven and in overalls, and in my disbelief
and astonishment I had not moved. I now invited her in, took
her coat, showed her to a place on the bench at my table. I set
about brewing some tea, and when it was ready, we sat and
drank tea and talked as we had done so often in the past, but in a
place I could least have imagined. She told me she knew this
part of the country well and that she had been around it quite a
bit when she lived at Skagen and wrote *Out of Africa*. She felt
that it was a very long time since we were last together and
asked if I would never again come to Rungstedlund. "You don't
need to say anything now, but could you not just come as in the
old days?" she asked. "Then we will not talk about all the sad
things at all but about something entirely different. I think we
have much to talk about; there are several things I would like to
ask you. I miss you, and it could be so enjoyable. Don't you
think so too?" At that moment, it was impossible for me to do
anything but agree, and then she slowly and in a bittersweet
manner said, slightly paraphrasing Schubert's "Faith in Spring"
(*Frühlingsglaube*), "Some time everything *must* take a turn for
the better."

She asked what I was working on, and when I had explained a
bit about it, she said that she had read my recently published
poem "The Sorcerers on Troll Skerry" (*Sejdmaendene paa Skratteskaer*). "I think it is a beautiful poem, a great poem," she said,
"but there is nevertheless something amiss about it, something
that is not quite as it should be. I have been thinking especially
of Øivind standing there tied to the skerry while the water is
rising around him. Why have you not let him think about how
it came to pass that the darkness he conjured up to fall upon

King Olav and his men instead fell upon him and his own men. That I do not understand; a storyteller would have let him think about it. I would have let him think about it; he definitely would have had to. That is the reason for his misfortune, and given such a long time for his thinking, it is inevitable that he will reflect on why it happened that way with the darkness: Why did it fall upon him and not on the king? Had we discussed it, you might have included that in the poem."

It struck me that she was right, and I agreed that this question is raised only twice in the poem, when the sorcerers are angry and ponder the derision they have been subjected to, derision which concerns the misplaced darkness that had blinded them. And I agreed with her that this in itself was a great theme that I had not seen, but that my oversight was perhaps due to the other things that so definitively constituted the focal point for me, and that there is an attention that selects and a distraction that excludes. I defended myself a bit in order not to succumb to the regret that I had not had it pointed out to me or seen it myself. I honestly found her thoughts fascinating, and suddenly, for a moment, I bitterly felt the loss of our conversations. "Yes, in a story I would have placed the emphasis on it," she said, "but I am sure that is because I *am* a storyteller and you are a lyric poet and hence must be more engrossed in the ego and what happens to it than in the events about it and beyond it. Perhaps that is also why we sometimes have such a difficult time because you observe to a lesser degree what takes place around you than what goes on inside you. But I suppose a lyric poet has to be like that."

After she had developed a philosophy of the story in "The Cardinal's First Tale," which she had given me to read long before, she had begun to tease me about the limitations and self-centered quality of the lyric poet as compared to the scope of the storyteller, who always sees more and includes more than himself, a characterization, subtle and pointed, in which everything depends on the shading of the syntax, in which she, of course, was the master. At the beginning of our friendship, she had made me feel that it was great and glorious to be a lyric poet, and she had often emphasized that the lyric poem was the acme of verbal art and perhaps of all art. Gradually the lyricist's art had been depreciated as something dubious and second best, the most hermetic and self-centered of the arts. Despite the general aim of her deliberations, I could not help hearing, nor escape feeling, that the lyric poet had to be me, and that the change in her evaluation had to be due to the disappointing acquaintance with the lyricist as a human being. When she got to the difference between the lyric poet and the storyteller, an unmistakable bitterness would come through, as it did when she spoke of the titans as opposed to the gods. Although she tried to hide it, that same bitterness came through now.

While we sat and talked and drank tea, the weather had changed back and forth between sunshine and heavy showers, between a sudden forenoon darkness and the dazzling reflection from the sea. When it cleared up about noon, she asked me to escort her to her hotel and get her a taxi because she had a luncheon engagement. We left the house and walked the narrow, winding sand path behind the dunes along the shore. As I walked ahead and now and then talked over my shoulder, I barely noticed a large snake—a viper—lying on the wet path in the cold sunlight, hissing and not moving away. We walked respectfully around it, eventually reaching the hotel, and got the only cab in Kandestederne.

The shock of her unexpected appearance had stayed with me during the first part of our conversation and slowly stabilized afterward into a feeling of bitter alienation and embarrassment which I overcame only sporadically. When she emphasized that she had come the long way solely for my sake, I could not remain untouched and bring myself to say that I wished she had not done it. Neither could I without contempt for myself, after all that I had thought and decided, receive her as if everything were fine.

As I walked back to the cottage, the feeling of the visit's unreality grew on me. Karen Blixen had now and then half seriously threatened to haunt me after her death to see what I was doing. In my exaggerated despair, I accepted her remark as a foretaste that I should never get outside her spell and power, that at whatever outermost ocean her "right hand would hold me," and that I should never again become as I once was: far better to be slow-witted, hesitant, and dependent on my own power, my own wings. And all this—combined with the thought of the snake we had seen, which had evoked the deepest discomfort in me, contrary to what I normally would feel— made me believe that that serpent would always lie in one place or another on our path. Its presence had affected me like a sign, something you are looking for when you do not know what is going on in yourself. Karen Blixen looked for signs more than anyone. She also did this time, as I was to discover later.

When I finally got back after walking for a long while along the ocean, I lay down on the bench and stared at the ceiling. All the progress, all the good results and the peace with myself I had gained by my resolute long solitude had blown away. I found it fundamentally unreasonable, foolish, and strangely heartless to oppose the generous and trusting attitude she had shown by coming to see me. I felt the sweetness of giving in overtake and relax me and I fixed my attention on her situation, trying to see everything through her eyes, and asking myself why there was this hysteria, why I could not see her and talk with her in all friendliness, and what would that cost me anyway? "Life itself is what it would cost you," something within me shouted back, and with no reasoning to back it up. A note from that time shows my vacillation: "This demonic play-acting penetrates all the nooks and crannies of existence itself, laughs uproariously in holy places, but takes its mask and its fame seriously, speaks of divine things with splendid gestures, and costumed like Pierrot disavows them with a shrug. She demands that the rules of tragedy be kept by everyone and reserves the satirical play for herself—behind the mask of tragedy, and yet, in spite of all that, she is Pellegrina." And so my thoughts and feelings wandered from one extreme to the other and began to dissolve one into the other in the days that followed until, prompted by sheer self-preservation, I finally saw clearly that I would have to pull myself together and not only make the break, but also inflict on Karen Blixen the degree of hurt and pain it would take to make it effective, which I had shied away from thus far out of consideration for her, or perhaps out of cowardice. And I decided to write a letter since it had become evident that silence was of no avail; so on September 15, 1954, I wrote:

Dear Baroness,

Since your visit here I have not had one hour's peace day or night, and both the star-filled skies and my work have become closed to me because I have been false to you and false to myself. And, without absolute truthfulness, I feel that I cannot take a single step forward. What good is it that I would like to renew our friendship and visit Rungstedlund again, when the pure mighty wilderness about me with all its voices cries out, No, No, No. . . . I wish that I were wiped off the surface of the earth because I let myself become so surprised and confused by the situation that I was unable to give the true answer immediately. There was a time in the past when I felt that I should die if I had to leave you; now I feel that I shall die if I return. It is not a conventional conscience that rebels, but my demon that revolts. I have ceased to think about the reasons; I only know that if I do not obey my demon, I shall be honest neither to you nor to myself and my life will lose all serious direc-

tion. And until this letter is posted I cannot close again
the circle I have drawn about myself and return to my
work. There the decisions await me and I have not, as
you may think, given up the divine for the superhuman. But I believe that only on a basis of complete
inner freedom does one find the way that leads to it—
and without absolute truthfulness in the perception of,
in the experience of, the divine I prefer to stick with
human nature and not let myself get carried away by
my desires.

I shall never forget my first evenings in the green
room enveloped by Tschaikovsky's autumnal violin
strains, which evoked all one's dreams or Haydn's sweet
rhythmic melody that made one trust in the future.
Then I felt security and protection, homecoming and
shelter, hidden away from the world, a convalescence
secure from all long-standing mistakes, at last in the
company of one knowing and wise. I was filled with a
new expectation, and the air was charged mysteriously
with a challenging demand, as for a feast, a creation, a
destiny. I can never be thankful enough for that.

You constituted for me a stretch of the road to the
divine and finally you have, involuntarily and in the
most awesome way, given me the inner freedom necessary to continue on that road. Do not take the gift back
now! If what happened was necessary, then this is also
necessary. Do not deprive me of the freedom I have paid
for with such pain, but set me free even beyond that—
or you will be using, or misusing, for your own purposes that vessel for the divine which you have been
for me in those wonderful hours. I have felt—and the
weather around me has borne out this feeling with un-
failing voice—that if I returned, I would lose the possibility of truthfulness and would be unfaithful to myself.

But only if our parting holds shall I have the premonition of a possible real reconciliation, and only then will the best that we have had be given back to me in memory like an autumn of meditative fullness, an earnest eternal spring.

I will it this way—because I must! And only then can I thank you again.

The day after I posted the letter, I received one from Karen Blixen; our letters had crossed. Her letter was destroyed, I believe, in accordance with her wishes, but I recall its contents fairly well. It was a great relief that I had already written and posted my letter, because hers was beautiful and cordial. She said that she had been very glad to visit me and see me in my new workplace and that if I had been slightly more hospitable, she would have stayed for lunch because the journey to see me had been long and tiring. But she thought that from now on all would be well, and that we could see each other with joy and that she had taken our encounter with the viper as a sign offered by her world, a serpent of brass that would protect us and our friendship against all evil.

The following day I received a second letter from Karen Blixen; it read: "Have received your letter, burn mine." With that, everything, including the finale, was over, and there was a great stillness in the universe. One may wonder why it had all been so difficult. The best explanation may be found in this quotation from *Out of Africa*: "There is this about witchcraft, that when it has once been practiced on you, you will never completely rid yourself of it."

On April 17, 1955, Ole Wivel and his wife gathered together for dinner a number of the friends and admirers of Karen Blixen to celebrate her seventieth brithday. Because she was ill, she herself did not attend but on the radio that evening sent her greetings and read her story "The Cloak." Each person at the dinner sent a special greeting to her. Mine, in the sonnet form that I knew she admired, evoked the magic of Rungstedlund. I sent her a copy of it.

That autumn *Anubis*, the collection of poems that I had worked so hard to complete, was published. At the time I was in Uppsala, studying at the Karolina Library for my dissertation. That autumn also I received word that my friend was engaged to be married to another man. It was as if there had been a pause in time and a deep silence. I was almost always alone and did nothing but read and take notes and once in a while listen to sacred music. A last hidden hope had been crushed when I heard of my friend's engagement, and now I was free of that involvement also. I lived in a room on the outskirts of the city. "The moon shines through the sheer curtains, as in Bonn," I thought that night. That also was behind me.

I sent *Anubis* to Karen Blixen with the following dedication:

Accept my greetings, accept my book—
It was here my demon, in deep dialogue,
First heard his language from human lips.

An intimacy only dreams can give,
Burning midnight oil in the silent house,
In close touch only with the stars and sea.

And if the rewards were mutual wrongs—
Again I remember, again I see,
And thank you for my anguish and my bliss.

One night I came home late, and as I opened the door to my room, I was greeted by the heavy fragrance of roses. When I switched the light on, I found an enormous bouquet of dark red roses, which my landlady had arranged in the largest vase in the apartment, with thanks and greetings from Karen Blixen. That same night I dreamt of her and saw her as she had been when we had our best times together, but the loud cannonlike boom of ice breaking up in the ocean below my window interrupted my dream. I awoke and for a long while lay musing in the darkness. I thought of Brittany and of the parting of spirits; a phase of my life—a fantastic and profound interlude—was over at last.

ECHOES

S O ENDS the story of my friendship with Karen Blixen. In *Last Tales*, published in the fall of 1957, she put down her version of our friendship in her story "Echoes." It is said that it was generally known in literary circles that the story is about our time together and that Emanuele is a portrait of me. If, as Parmenia Migel writes in her book *Titania: The Biography of Isak Dinesen*, the portrait was regarded as "a kind of *cause célèbre*," I was ignorant of it, being far too occupied with other matters. But Karen Blixen herself was very eager that people who had known of our close relationship should also know that "Echoes" was her depiction of it. That she wanted the fact to go down in literary history is evident in this passage from Robert Langbaum's study of Karen Blixen's art:

> We can learn from "Echoes" how Isak Dinesen turns life into art, because the story is based—she was anxious to have me know this—on an incident in her life. According to her account, she grew interested in the early 1950's in a young Danish poet of the circle that published *Heretica*, a literary magazine of which she was a patron. The young poet became her protégé and friend, and would come for long periods to work at Rungstedlund. But then, fearful that she was gaining too much influence over him, the young man turned against her with a suddenness and violence that shattered her. The break between them, which occurred in 1954, is the experience behind "Echoes."

Only my name is lacking, but that was supplied later in Parmenia Migel's book, along with a description of the events in

greater detail.* "A long chapter might well be written by some
future literary analyst," said Parmenia Migel, "about the sway
Tania had over him and its consequences for both of them." I
have now done that to the best of my ability, and what it lacks in
objectivity is perhaps counterbalanced by firsthand knowledge.
And since Karen Blixen has referred so carefully to the concrete
background for her story, it would seem not unreasonable, on
that account alone, that the other party also present his view.

"Echoes" is Karen Blixen's final answer to me. Strongly com-
pacted, it truly presents, as if in code, what happened between
us. I might add: it is based on false premises, but comes to a
correct conclusion. There is but a hint of my love affair, so
fraught with consequences, and in the story it has no influence
whatever on the course of events.

As in the Cloak trilogy, the events in "Echoes" have been
placed in Italy; but while in the former they consist of freely
developed, fantastic variations on a theme, the concrete merely
a touch, in the latter they form part of a real *roman à clef*. One of
the boy's decisive remarks during his confrontation of Pellegrina
is taken almost verbatim from my last letter to Karen Blixen:
"Once I thought that I should die if I were to leave you. Now I
know that I should die if I went back to you." In the letter the
continuation was: "It is not a conventional conscience that rebels, but my demon that revolts." In "Echoes" she held on to the
first part and ignored the second. (Demon, here, as in my
dedicatory poem, is, of course, to be taken in the Greek sense of
a consulting and guiding inner voice.)

In "Echoes" there are several other hidden quotations from
our time together, such as "Remember—only the hard things
ring," the characterization of laughter, and "Dear child, come
to me," from *"Erlkönig,"* in the sense she had used it to tease

* Parmenia Migel's book appeared seven years before *The Pact*. The latter is
discussed at length sympathetically in Judith Thurman's *Isak Dinesen: The Life
of a Storyteller* (New York: St. Martin's Press, 1982). —Tr.

me. All of these call attention to the story as an answer to me, concentrated in Pellegrina's thoughts at the end, where she sits at the watering trough after she has washed and wiped away the bloodstains from their showdown. The words preceding this painfully beautiful exit, uttered to me across all misunderstandings and mistakes, are: "Oh my child, dear Brother and Lover. Be not unhappy, and fear not. It is all over between you and me. I can do you no good and I shall do you no harm."

"Echoes" is in many ways a very beautiful story. I love in particular the beginning, where Pellegrina arrives in the quiet, cool autumn in the mountains, a wonderful opening to a sudden high point, and the sadly jarring discord that no reconciliation can dissolve. The disappointment was too great for that in real life and it is, uncurtailed and unchanged, stamped directly onto the story. Apart from the quotations, everything in it is paraphrased and changed, but the disappointment is locked in, traumatic and unchanged: the world and I shall know it, its bitterness and immensity.

It had been very important to Karen Blixen to place our relationship primarily on the level of art and to place me as a student there, although in the beginning she wanted to teach me to live, through travel and through love, and not to concern myself with writing poetry. I have learned practically nothing about my art, its lyric skill, from her. Only late in our relationship did she try to give me some lessons, but she did teach me about life, which, of course, has given me a strong impulse to write. Although she seldom acted wisely, it was precisely her wisdom that I learned from—and from her folly which also was greater than most, when it unscrupulously made use of her wisdom. But from the beginning in "Echoes" the issue is art, and to obtain the maximum isolated and purebred talent to relate to, she has separated the sex and the voice, exactly as they are in the eunuch and the choirboy. Thus she has also separated the human quality and the talent, in order thereafter to dream of a human quality that in some wonderful way is identifiable with the talent. Only then can the disappointment in the unknown X, in Emanuele's human qualities, become astonishing and immense. The disappointment is in his cowardice and in his sensitivity, physical as well as mental. She never reproved me for the former to my face, but abundantly for the latter. Apart from the teasing in it that I know so well, the physical side of it, like certain passages of the tale, probably is meant to stand for the mental aspect. I refused to play enough or to play properly with her.

The disappointment was real, but why was it so great? When the unforeseen—life she did not know and the course of which she could not calculate in advance—occurred and moved her deeply (the breach of the laws of history which again and again is the theme in her tales), the grief of the loss of Africa, the farm, and Denys Finch-Hatton welled up in her and with it a demand and an expectation so great and intense that only disappointment could follow. It was almost as if she were under compulsion, and yet also as if she had willed it herself, so that with a secret, terrified delight she had to relive her loss. For if she could no longer find her happiness, she could, in the words of Goethe, relive and repeat her happiness in her anguish.

Finally, Karen Blixen was probably predisposed, almost constitutionally, to disappointment. "The phenomena of life were not great enough for her; they were not in proportion with her own heart," she says about Pellegrina. There is no doubt that the repeated disappointments in her life were the price she paid for the power of her fantasy, whether it exerted itself in her art and created insight and structure, emotion and form there, or whether it stepped outside and desired something directly from life. If anything impeded the fulfillment of her wishes or if the events of life did not measure up to them, the road from insight to wish became the way of passion and witchcraft, the road of insight used magically, while the road from wish to insight, the diametric opposite, became the way of wisdom. The former ended blindly with misadventure, distress, and disappointment; the latter ended in the story.

There was no earthly way I could have satisfied the expectations that Karen Blixen did not conceal I had given rise to in her. I would have had to be a superman, a child of the gods, a genie, or a ghost not to disappoint her. Or, to stay with the image of "Echoes," a prodigious voice without a body, or, most desirable, a body and a mind without a history, and, as it happens with a great love, one reborn solely by meeting her, able to begin its history from that very moment. I should have forgotten my history, existentially excluded it from me; I was young enough to do that, while she remembered hers, which was remote enough not to disturb, and rich and extraordinary and fabulous enough to add an invaluable dimension to our relationship: the history from which she regained her identity and could advance and teach me, incessantly alternating between motherly, sisterly, and erotic love—the childless woman who wanted an heir, the lonely woman who wanted a lover. Regardless of the demonic teasings and the contemptuous attacks, these are great and beautiful elements that permeate the tale, and that, in farewell, make a lasting impression on me. By the full effort of creative generosity, she succeeded in overcoming the last feelings of resentment and revenge. I was probably not strong enough, but being what I was, I did what was possible and right for me, and I stand by it. Her exalted aim and her fundamental mistake, along with her knowledge of herself, are expressed in these lines in "Echoes," where Pellegrina thinks of Emanuele's feelings for music and his nature's musicality:

> She could not tell whether there was much more,
> neither could she tell whether she herself wished for
> more to be there. She had heard his voice before she had

heard his story; to her from the first the two had been
one, and his singer's career his vocation.

A mightier impetus to create, a more productive seduction, I
have not met in my life.

THE MOONLADY ⤸ ⤸ ⤸ ⤸ ⤸

THE fundamental dialogue between Karen Blixen and me, the one that she with all her will to mythologize (and that at times would turn into mythomania), that she did not rule or have at her disposal, concerned the problem of identity, the question: Who am I? Karen Blixen thought the answer was found in one's place in history understood as story, by accepting one's role in it with perfect obedience. I sought the answer in one's relation to the cosmos, by letting oneself be adjusted by it in perfect contemplative openness. I have expressed this fundamental view in my poem "The Raven" (*Ravnen*). The first section which I read to Karen Blixen during the early phase of our friendship, concerns a violent departure that seeks identity in cosmic connection, and with it the question "Who am I?" is set forth with all the energy of desperation. She never discussed the poem with me, but she gave an answer in "The Cardinal's First Tale" and let me know that it was her answer, the most forceful reply from her in our basic dialogue, the storyteller's answer. But she gave it in relation to something else, namely the novel, the modern novel, and not in relation to the universe, just as in "Echoes" she gave her answer in relation to the conventional conscience and fear of witches, and not to the inner demonic, guiding voice, the one that in "The Raven" leads to the cosmos and the determination of identity in relation thereto. The thought revolted her, but it lay outside the realm within which she would answer, namely that of the storyteller. Perhaps this was what she meant when she said that she was a storyteller and that I was a lyric poet.

"The Cardinal's First Tale" opens with the question: "Who are you?" and it ends with the statement that our identities are determined solely by our roles and places in a story; there is no other instance in the world that can answer the question of who we are. "For within our whole universe the story only has authority to answer that cry of heart of its characters, that one cry of heart of each of them: '*Who am I?*'" It is a brilliant reflection, as long as it pertains to the story, but if the story is made the only instance, the reflection goes beyond its validity; it is no longer correct. If it is extended to cover life itself, for example, it becomes disastrously wrong. The view quite naturally underlies Karen Blixen's work, in which two tales, "The Poet" and "The Immortal Story," are both, although in different ways, about the folly of trying to apply the laws of the story to life itself. But while she was occupied with the problem of identity and of bringing the philosophy of the story into consciousness, the insight was repressed so thoroughly that it now sounds as if the story rightfully and definitely should take over from life: "In the beginning was the story. At the end we shall be privileged to view and review it—and that is what is named the day of judgment."

That it has gone that far is without doubt because toward the end of her life it gradually became vital for Karen Blixen to resolve the question of identity. She had approached the answer early in her writings, clearly in "The Revenge of Truth," but only later on and here in "The Cardinal's First Tale" does it reach its completion. In her rendering of situations of crisis, we see how the identity and the life of will and desire connected with it either is given up—so that alternating desires and wills without constancy run through the person—or the identity is adhered to, while the life of will and desire connected with it is liquidated forever so that the identity, so to speak, becomes empty, a convention, a formalism. We see the former happen to Pellegrina, the latter to Alkmene and Adelaide. For Pellegrina the gate between her ego and life has once and for all time been lifted off its hinges and whirled away; for Alkmene and Adelaide the gate has become jammed beyond repair. After the life-nerve is hit, the one person will not play a single part, but many parts; the others will play none at all. Their problems have created the tales in which they are the principal characters, but the tales have in no way solved their problems of identity.

The solution comes with the philosophy of the story as Karen Blixen drafts it in "The Cardinal's First Tale," and from the moment she becomes conscious of that philosophy it is extended to cover life itself. At this point, unaware of her own wishes and their fusion with her new consciousness, she is constrained to repeat the theme from "The Poet": the Councilor's cast of characters corresponds, to the same extent as the events in "Echoes," to what really took place between us. Her disappointment and scorn because I would not submit to God's plan and to certain concepts of honor clearly turned into disappointment and indignation because I would not play the part in the story which she, not I, knew and thought I was cast in. I believed in no such story; I wanted to relate directly to the cosmos, where no hand would guide me or hold me fast, to use the distorted quotation from the Bible, a hand I increasingly felt to be the Councilor's, the puppeteer's, hers; and the more firmly I stood for my freedom to do it, the more firmly she stood for the laws of the story. Thus, from the moment our relationship turned into compulsion, it changed from a wonderful and creative dialogue of life into a painful and demonic, intimate and suffocating power struggle and religious dispute. The dispute centered on where we, in the last instance, should find our identity and learn who we were: whether it should take place in relation to the story or in relation to the cosmos.

We were in agreement that a third possibility existed, the tragic solution, as described in "Peter and Rosa," where the persons in an inextricable situation, in accord with nature and with God's plan, living to the full, hold on to their identities and die with them. That creates the tale; it is not a pattern, a divine work of man, bestowed in advance.

Both Karen Blixen and I speak of the cosmos in the same sense. Yet there is a decisive difference. Karen Blixen's perception of nature is sublime and deep, her life with nature intense and wonderful. I know of nothing more beautiful and more knowing, unsentimental and precise; but for her the cosmos is everywhere experienced and perceived through nature and the elements, while to my mind's eye nature and the elements are integrated into the cosmos and perceived through it. There is more to this modest shift of emphasis than one would think at first. Her starting point in nature made her relation to God so personal, so anthropomorphic, that it repeatedly turned into self-glorification and frequently led her to exercise power as if she were herself a goddess. One could feel awe, but also horror, with regard to this brilliant madness. One could only give in to it or get out of its way. From this came her inhuman loneliness in spite of friends and relatives, publicity and fame. I do not think that she recognized one living person as her equal except Denys Finch-Hatton.

Twenty years ago, just after my definitive parting from Karen Blixen, I received a request to write about her. It was worded in such a way that it was difficult for me to refuse. But I answered on October 3, 1954, as follows:

> Just a few weeks ago I broke off my relationship with Karen Blixen, a decision that has thrown me into difficult, troubled thoughts, profound doubt and sorrow, but also one that has brought a sense of relief, of breathing the air of truth again after a long spell.
>
> Under the circumstances I feel that it is incumbent upon me to keep a promise I once made to Karen Blixen: Not to write about her until after her death.

I made her that promise at the height of our friendship, and later, at our best moments, she had taken it up and expounded upon it: "You shall not write about me until after I have died. But then you must. You will, then, be completely free and will not be concerned with what I would think of what you say. If I were alive, I would be unable to refrain from meddling, and that I would rather not do. Perhaps I could not stand reading it, perhaps I would think it was wonderful, but write entirely from your heart, write as you wrote in your sonnets on Nietzsche. I do wish you would do that." She said this in one of her open, confident, and gay periods, when she reached back to her first wish, that I should act as freely as if she did not exist. And then, with a sweeping calm as if Elysium were something she experienced here and now, she concluded by saying that nothing I had done or would do could harm our friendship.

It did not turn out that way. But after twenty years I finally feel that I have enough strength to understand that friendship not from its end but from its beginning and to put down how wonderful and yet full of risk it was. I have endeavored to do so according to the words of Goethe:

> *Sag nur nichts halb:*
> *Ergänzen, welche Pein!*
> *Sag nur nichts grob:*
> *Das Wahre spricht sich rein.*

> (Say not just half of it:
> To complete it, what pain!
> Say nothing gross:
> The truth speaks clean.)

Karen Blixen worshiped the moon, and in an ancient ritualistic manner regarded the coming of the new moon as an opportunity for renewal. She therefore reverently curtsied to it. Quite frankly and literally she considered herself to be of its kind and to have a part in its power. Such a belief is outside the current realm of experience in our civilization, and it is the formula for her relationship with the cosmic movements in nature. "The elements that are truly sensitive to the moon must live with that fact or forgive it that it pulls them in with so strong a rhythm"—Karen Blixen had sent me that message when I was in Brittany. By the moon she meant in this case herself. What sharpened my recollection from day to day in writing of our friendship, what I shall recall when all else is forgotten, is that enormous attraction.